FUNNY YOU SHOULD SAY THAT!

FUNNY YOU SHOULD SAY THAT!

MY JOURNEY INTO GIFT, PURPOSE AND CONSCIOUSNESS

T. Brandon Russ

gatekeeper press™

Columbus, Ohio

Funny You Should Say That! My Journey Into Gift, Purpose and Consciousness

Published by Gatekeeper Press
2167 Stringtown Rd, Suite 109
Columbus, OH 43123-2989
www.GatekeeperPress.com

The cover design and editorial work for this book are entirely the product of the author. Gatekeeper Press did not participate in and is not responsible for any aspect of these elements.

Library of Congress Control Number: 2022948582

ISBN (paperback): 9781662932977

I was in the same seat as many of those in this book and even the people reading this now. When it came time to deliver a message to me, Brandon simply said, "Your Grandfather says get the damn tattoo." Things changed for me that day, as it had for many others who got their loved one back in just one sentence.

Shortly after that event we were told, "Two weeks to flatten the curve." During the pandemic shut down, I took every class Brandon had to offer. I was in his "Covid Class," the first remote Intuitive Development class he taught via Zoom. When the restrictions were finally lifted and we were able to meet again in person, I would frequent the shop for a Smokey Quartz or a Carnelian, and attended every message circle and class being offered. Brandon asked me to help with the shop on the weekends due to my love for crystals and all things metaphysical. I became the "Crystal Concierge." While working at the shop and continuing classes, Brandon asked me to go on the road for his "Bring Them Back to Life Tour." My role was to assist and introduce him at the top of show.

"Me? Sandy?" The girl who has never held a microphone? Introduce a Medium at a sold-out show? There are two things Brandon and Spirit have in common. They see the bigger plan and they know what they are doing. Me, Sandy, the girl who now holds the mic and introduces Medium T. Brandon Russ in front of hundreds of people, learned to be seen and heard. I guess Brandon and Spirit got it right.

To this day my best introduction is, "Hi, I'm Sandy. I have studied under Brandon for a year a half now, studying everything from Intuitive Development to Mediumship. Now, I'm standing here in this Saloon with a wine slushie talking to all of you. Well, what I am trying to say is, make better life decisions. Here's Brandon."

All jokes aside, I treated each event as a workshop while staying in the moment. I was there to witness many of the moments in this book. I can tell you, "Yes they really happened and yeah, he's the real deal." Every event and every reading are all completely different but all have a commonality. That of healing and humor.

What I am trying to say is, "Here's Brandon."

Funny You Should Say That!

Many books about Mediums start out with the tale of how they were suddenly struck by an affliction, tragedy or even a lightning strike. I hope you do not expect that here. I mean, although I saved a bus full of orphans from careening down a bridge embankment with nothing more than my intuition and expensive sneakers, does not mean I have superpowers. As a matter of fact, I did not stop the bus and save those orphans. Nope. I'm a regular guy. I think my gifts and ability come naturally and stem from who I am, the circumstances, conversations, and inspiration I have for others. I was packaged in a white male with average features, and born into an Irish Catholic, middle class family that had a wicked sense of humor. Yep, you were either funny or you 'got run over with the funny,' as my grandmother used to say.

When I set out on this part of my path, I had to recognize that everything mattered. All the careers I had, the experiences I been a part of and most importantly, my personality needed to be a key part of it. Reason being, I was always getting in trouble or becoming frustrated because of the way I acted. I ultimately had to make myself want to be happy every day. My nature, my delivery, my essence has always been about humor. Even when I needed to have difficult conversations, I always did it with a funny tale or even better, I would come off completely inappropriate. I was often misunderstood but was the resident 'fun guy' that always kept things light. I knew I needed to combine my gifts with who I was and what I was passionate about. I had to find my groove of delivery and what my mission would be, because after being a six figure corporate guy, I needed a mission.

One of the primary challenges I saw in myself was that I always stayed in a comfort zone. Every one of my career moves was from one middle class, white male-centric situation to another. I literally got the job because I fit the mold they were looking for. Well spoken, educated and demographically appealing. I can't tell you the exact day it hit me, but when it did, I realized what a sham I felt like. With 15 years' experience in the recruiting industry, I can tell you, the game is this, schmooze the clients and move people from one broken, marginal situation to another. Negotiate worth or value and be the voice for people that don't have the courage or skills to speak for themselves. They didn't the 'in' that I had because I had an expense account. Nope. It was a horrible existence, and I died every day while in the seat. I weighed over 400 pounds and used to stop and eat fast food on my way home to eat dinner, before going out for ice cream and stay up late for a midnight snack. I might have been the jovial guy, but I hated myself. Not in the Sylvia Plath sort of way, but rather in the frustrated, there must be more to life than this sort of way.

A new development has occurred...

I did a deeper dive into WHO I was. The message came to me, literally. I had a business friend that asked me to lunch. Someone asking if you were available for coffee or lunch was code for 'get me out of my job'. Recruiters know this and budget for it. I arrived at the restaurant and we sat in the back. She had a prominent business networking position, so EVERYONE knew her. She had asked for the back room as it was not affected by the lunch rush. All normal things to recruiter with a new candidate. What happened next changed the course of my history.

"I'm leaving my job," she said abruptly.

I knew it was coming in some way, but she really cut to the chase. I asked how I could help her, thinking she'd had a Jerry McGuire moment, held up her goldfish and said, "who's coming with me?"

"I wanted to tell you something that's been happening with me." I was a little worried I was going to get a Multi-Level-Marketing pitch. "I've been taking classes for a few years and now I'm a certified Medium. I've been doing it on the down low for a few years and now I'm ready to do it full time."

I looked at her and it all made sense. At all the meetings we sat through, she was always saying two things at once. I completely understood what she was saying and most times, was the only one that understood.

"I want to talk to you about your mother in-law, Christine. You are completely crestfallen about losing her and she needs you to get going."

I looked at her with the same look anyone that has been intruded upon would have. But my need to understand the last 30 seconds of dialog and hearing that my mother-in-law was coming through, was almost too much. Almost.

"You drive her car, don't you? The clothes in the trunk need to be dropped off. You told everyone you did it weeks ago. You need to let go, she's not here."

I think I ordered something. That is to say, I remember eating cold fries at the end of our time. I sat there and listened to her deliver a SPECIFIC message about my loss, my fears and what I needed to hear about getting my ass in gear. She invited me to take classes that she was offering on Psychic Development. Her final sales pitch at the end was simple, "It is all right there, your ability, I see it clearly. You want to make people smile, be happy. Understand how you work and come to the class. If you do not like it, you don't have to keep coming."

One of the greatest gifts I've had in this journey has been to have her influence and watching her 'make it.' I attended those classes and my gift only grew with each session. I attended her first demonstration and saw her deliver to a room of people. She was *spot on* all evening. At the end of the event, she came around to the tables and thanked people for coming. As she left my table, she turned me loose. "You guys are in for a treat. Brandon is one of my best students. He's going to give you all a reading."

What, the what?

I had delivered lots of messages…in class. Class was such a safe place. Everyone knows each other and they are open. Nope, not now, no training wheels, net or Amethyst in sight. I just let it rip, as they say. I might have hit about 50% in the 20-minute barrage of nervous energy I spewed on them. But I needed to learn. I needed to learn that I wasn't just meant to develop this ability, this gift, this running coincidence of my words, I was meant to USE my gift. She encouraged me in that moment and for a lifetime. Sometime after that event, she pulled me aside after class and let me in on things. "You know you are supposed to do this in your life path, right?" I had to HEAR the message instead of subtly putting it together.

You notice that I haven't named her. I won't. I respect her wishes to never use her name in developing and becoming who I am supposed to be. Whether or not she is willing to recognize my undying gratitude to her. This industry needs to recognize that we are all in it together to heal the way we are meant to. I wouldn't be where I am today without her and the experiences she shared with me. Every student, client, and message I connect with, began with her spark in me. For that, I am eternally grateful.

I went on to study with a past life regressionist, Qi Gong master, Shaman and Reiki Masters. I have studied with Buddhists and Franciscans. None had as much impact as my first teacher in this work. The spark turned to flame and is now a fire that I share with others. That is impact. I, Thank you.

You Miss Your Grandmother

'Coming out' about my ability had its challenges. From criticism by the elderly choir ladies that saw me grow up in Catholic Church as an altar boy, to the graduating class of Shaker 1991. Some of the class may or may not have seen me jump from a roof in my underwear and a Vikings helmet into Johnny Finnigan's pool while his parents were away in Europe.

So, when I was contacted by someone I knew well back in high school, she had to get past the comedic and not take anything seriously attitude. She knew me when I had hair out to there and down my back, "Livin' on a Prayer" and always making a joke. I knew she married a guy she met in college named Shmalsky, and had a couple of kids. She sent me a message and asked me if I really was a Medium.

"Are you like a Medium, Medium? As in like a real, you know, Medium?"

I responded, "Well, I'm more of an extra-large, but yes, I am a Medium."

"LOL. You haven't changed... But seriously, how would I get an appointment?"

"Well, here's my info and I'd be honored to read you."

"Oh, no, it's not for me... It's for my husband. He had a loss a few years ago and he never really got over it."

"Oh, very cool. I'm glad you trust me that way."

I never heard from him.

I told you that part of story, to tell you this one. I passionately believe that your message is coming. The challenge is whether you are paying attention or take the opportunity to acknowledge a sign from a loved one. They are there, you just have to pay attention.

Just because you have a high sense of intuition and connection, does not mean you know all and see all. Like for instance, where the police are hiding. On a beautiful sunny day in suburbia upstate New York, I got pulled over at 9:30 in the morning.

As I waited for the officer to saunter up to my window, all I could think of was the inconvenience of the whole thing. It's going to be on Wednesday night, it's going to be $300, I'm going to sit there like a perp and so on. I was flustered by the time he arrived.

"Do you know why I pulled you over?"

"Because you miss your grandmother?" I said without hesitation.

The look on his face was that of stunned and slightly offended. Remember, this is a man that has a gun, a taser and a baton, and I just called out his grandmother. Flabbergasted, he grabbed my license and registration from me and marched off. I kind of knew that I shouldn't have said it.

Then my thoughts turned to, "Oh no, now who can I call for bail, this is going to be $1,000, I'm not going to do well in prison." I seriously thought my time with freedom was close to an end. But the officer was remarkably calm when he returned.

"Listen, you have a clean record and all, but you have to take it easy through here." He handed back my stuff and I saw the smirk come across his face. "But I gotta ask you. Funny you should have asked that. Why did you say that to me when I asked why you thought I pulled you over?"

"Well…" I let the pause be as pregnant as a captured audience would allow. The thoughts raced through me as I checked myself for a moment. Was I *really* about to give a cop that pulled me over a reading in broad daylight?

"… Here is my card," I started. "I'm a Medium and there is woman standing behind you on your mother's side. She makes it very clear that she is proud of you and she loves that she can see you in uniform because she never got the chance." I was simple and matter of fact about it. He stood there with the skeptic mic drop that happens often when people don't see it coming.

"She also appreciates that you ask her to protect you every shift. She's proud that you remember her and she has your back. She will always make sure you return for your children, you know the ones in the picture on the dashboard, every day."

His eyebrows were raised up as he listened. His lips parted with a stutter and he simply said, "How?"

He regained his composure as he continued, "She died right after I graduated from academy. She passed just before I started this job. And I talk to her every day, I know she hears me, I just know it. I ask her to protect me. Every day."

I saw the human side of what the blue shield is every day. I sensed his pride, his fear and his determination for Country and family. It was a humbling experience, to see a grown man be brought to the edge of tears, vulnerable and in the position of power. He was judicious as he very easily could have given me a ticket for parking on the pavement (ahem). I knew I needed to lighten this situation up.

"And listen, she also thinks you don't need to pull over middle aged men in blue minivans on Route 9 on a Tuesday morning."

He looked at me with a laugh and he thanked me. I told him that he can call me any time, but I knew he wouldn't. As he turned to leave, I saw his name tag, "Shmalsky." He was the husband of the person I went to high school with that never called me for a reading.

Your message is coming. Ready or not.

Before I get too far ahead of myself, it's probably a good idea to explain how I realized, I was meant to be a Medium. There were plenty of trials and errors, along with experience and lessons. I always longed for something big and was never satisfied with anything. I could never just be happy. Not in any job, or any situation. One thing I am proud of, is that I went through it, I didn't go around it. If there were rewards, I took them. If there were lessons, I learned them. I realized I needed to master my energy.

This is what that journey and book is about. My journey on how I learned how to become what I was meant to be, in whatever moment the Universe put me in.

Newport, 1969

W as there anything sexier than a sailor in port? According to my mother, no. Terry was born and raised Catholic and went from one all-girls school to the other. So, by the time she got to Salve Regina (an all-girls college in Newport), she was ready to run away and join the Hell's Angels because the next stop after graduation was a nunnery. Not that my father wasn't a fine choice. The coincidence that she went to all-girls college in a port town, and that they got married relatively quickly, tells me she wasn't just settling down, she was stepping out of where she came from.

My dad took the natural and almost obvious route into the Navy. He was one of nine kids from Minnesota. Just before he turned 18, he was headed for the high seas. Adventure, opportunity and most likely, warm weather. Nate saw every opportunity to have fun, a true Sagittarius. He continues to be the life of the party with dad jokes, the master of ceremonies and the one to be quick with entertainment.

They swear they waited until marriage, but it doesn't stop me from doing the math every anniversary, being the first born. Being the son of two fire signs, an Aries and Sagittarius, ending up a water sign in Pisces seems like a tough lot. I am a Leo rising and it is a saving grace. When I compare our three charts, I understand where my strengths and weaknesses came from. It was an important part of my realization to who I am and how

I was made. If we are made from the stars then our astrology is everything.

After they were married, my dad had to finish out his commitment to the Navy and they were stationed in Norfolk, Virginia. I was born at Portsmouth Naval Hospital. My Pisces angle is 11' 11. My Leo rising and Aquarius moon give me the balance, the drive and the purpose to change the world around me. That's where the strange and often bizarre circumstances found me. A few days after I was born, I went missing. It wasn't because an of overdeveloped motor skill, it was because they thought my mom had postpartum depression. In the wisdom of the military, it was to keep the child from their mother. The family story is that it was only for a day or so. But I sensed and saw it longer. I was returned without incident. But a month later, I returned to the hospital because of the medical term, "failure to thrive." I simply wasn't eating. I received last rites and given a low percentage rate of survival. Without fail, I made a complete and unexplained comeback. I was back home within days and never looked back.

Years later, I was on a social media page about Alien Contact (CE-5). In a page building post, someone did a roll call to see where we were in the world. For no reason, people started added in their current location as well as their birthplace. There were more than a handful that cited Norfolk, particularly the naval hospital. Then someone said they were a Medium. In all, there were eight of us that were born between 1971-1974 and had an eerily similar story about going missing, failing to thrive and then, wait for it… all were working Mediums. Puts a whole new meaning to the term "Navy Brat."

Before I was born, my mom was a biology major and had a job at none other than the Edgar Cayce Institute. She was essentially stuffing pill bottles that promoted the nutrition that Cayce felt we needed, because the government had cross bred fruits and vegetables so much, that while the production of crops was amazing, it was sacrificing nutrients.

My mother's career before I was born was something I didn't learn about until I was over 45. I realized it was a piece of the puzzle. I had been obsessed with Cayce during my development. "The Sleeping Prophet" was an inspiration and a cautionary tale about how to use your gift properly. He was so accurate, down to the evidence. He would not only say that the client would need to drink from a blue bottle filled with an elixir, but he would also name the pharmacy, the town and the exact location on the shelf it would be located. His skills were more about remote viewing as much as it was spirit connection. He believed deeply in his dreams of Atlantis and how the return was both physical and symbolic.

I consider Cayce a teacher. For both the idea as to how he operated, but also how he learned about boundaries. These were very important to my own life path. Especially the parts of his path where he healed himself and listened to his own body. He had allowed the wrong people in and they took advantage of him and his gifts. That was a lesson I would have loved to learn vicariously. He became very sick because of it. He rebounded because he not only found his compass, but he found the right combination of spirit, purpose and gift. Not to mention delivery. I read his books, studied his approach and meditated on his lessons.

When my mom casually mentioned that she remembered being pregnant with me while she had a job at the Cayce Institute, you could have knocked me over with a feather. I had been a working Medium for over 10 years, and she brings this up in passing. Classic mom.

My parents always supported me in whatever crazy ideas I had. From driving an ice cream truck that sat in their driveway, to hearing me play drums for years on end. They simply wanted me to be happy. I was plenty of torture for my parents though, particularly my mom. It was in my soul contract to be radiant, outgoing, charming and a downright trouble maker. An angel with a tilted halo. It is her contract to field the phone calls from principles, sustain a judgmental glare and redirect me when I went off the rails. There was no shortage on how my connection with spirit and my abilities, would find their way into any situation, as I was simply a conduit.

Like the time I was in church on an ordinary Sunday. While the worship dance went on, I zoned. What I was actually doing was reading auras. I would see the light glow around everyone. Greens, yellows and blues. Good people feeling a part of a community while providing service to one another. One day I saw gray. Not black. Often misinterpreted, black is simply the absence of definition. When I saw gray, it shook me. Because gray means muddy, lost and disturbed. The loss of color. Vitality.

"Mrs. Miller doesn't look good, mom," my whisper could be heard in the choir loft.

The mom stare began with pursed lips as my dad ran cover with a cough. "Yeah, I'm going to miss her." I think a pin dropped as Mrs. Miller braced herself against the alter, because everyone heard me say it. One mission was accomplished that day, we were out of church before the organ stopped. My mom turned around from the front seat. "Why would you say that out loud?!?" Her voice was shrilly and her breathing huffy. My dad drove quickly out of the parking lot. I remember my dad talking out of the side of his mouth, "She sorta looks like shit, Terry."

I never saw Mrs. Miller again on the alter at church. But she sat next to me one day and told me she should have listened to me that day. I thanked her for being part of my path and told her I didn't mean to hurt her. She made it clear; I helped her, she just didn't listen. She told me, "You better go." I stood up and made my first communion.

That was about the same time that while sitting in class, I had a clear conversation with this beautiful woman that couldn't stop talking about my teacher. I had a full-on conversation right there in class and I'm sure I looked a little crazy with saying, "Oh yeah, I know," and "She's my favorite teacher," into the air.

"MR. RUSS please come up to my desk." Ms. Dorian was firm, yet kind. She was the type of person that was a safe space and you could share anything with. Even something embarrassing would not be off limits. "Who are you talking to?" she asked in calm voice over the desk.

"Mary Ellen… she said she was happy you are back in class today and she loves you too."

Her face went cold and she rushed out of the room. I felt her sorrow and pain. Minutes later, the secretary and principal were at the classroom door.

"MR. RUSS, please come to my office." Sister Mary Knucklepants did the best she could to try and hide her scowl. To accurately describe our relationship, it would be summarized with the word, disgusted. It may have been due to the time I brought in a giant jar of snakes on St. Patrick's Day. Jackie Hayes knocked it over and all the snakes slithered through the hallway. To the delight of the boys cheering them on and the screeches of the girls and nuns, I personally drove all the snakes out of St. Marie's school that day.

It might also have been because of the time I dressed like a nun for Halloween. Which seemed innocent enough until I slipped the pillow in under the dress and stood in front of the whole school and said, "Hey look at this… just like Mary!"

Being put on conference call in Sister Mary Knucklepants' office was old hat for me. So much so, I showed her how to click the buttons to put it on speaker and not lose the call. Tilted halo, I had.

"Hello Mrs. Russ, Sister Mary Knucklepants here with Brandon."

I sat back in my chair and started to cry. I didn't know what I had done wrong. The snake thing was good intention. The pregnant nun thing, ok, I went for the joke on that one. But here, it made me feel good until my teacher ran out of the room and I was being shamed for doing what I thought was kind. I told her good news. I told her she was loved. This paradigm didn't look at the dead the way they worshiped it.

My mom timidly admitted ownership. "What happened this time?" sounding like Harriet Nelson.

"Apparently Brandon told Mrs. Dorian that her mother was glad she was back in class and that she loves her too." Not following along, my mom asked for clarity.

"Mrs. Russ... Mrs. Dorian buried her mother last week, which is why she wasn't in school."

I don't think my mom knew what to say or do, other than to say she would get me right away. I remember the principal asking my mother, "What do you talk about at the dinner table?" and my mom finally got pissed. I also realized that how I use this gift affects everyone around me. I didn't realize how deeply or how far at that stage. But this was my first direct and clear communication with someone in passing. True Mediumship.

Santa Claus is an easy read

Spoiler alert before reading further. Your parents are Santa Claus. I repeat, the grownups buy things at stores so you can open them on Christmas morning. I was at that curious age where you are in the sweet spot of still fully believing in a jolly ole elf, and being made fun of for saying that you're being extra special good when Eric Cipowicz wants to throw snowballs at cars. It's profound when you realize that it was meant as a gentle lie to give you hope and to do good things, but later realize it was meant to control the rebellion you had raging inside you. Enough about the criminal intent of Christmas. Time to talk about the halcyon days of the rose-colored memories of what made your heart feel full, for even just a few days.

In the formative years, you become quite the super sleuth to find presents and snoop in all the usual hiding places. The closet, the attic and the crawlspace in the basement. But I was retired from that, because this year, I was being extra special good. Even my parents were amazed I had turned the corner. I was no longer curious. Little did they know, I simply already knew.

My dad likely took credit behind the scenes because he and I had the man to man talk. It wasn't about the birds and the bees. It was about believing in a fat man or getting nothing. See, I had two younger sisters, three and six years younger. I understood why he was protecting their experience, I really did. But I had a whole other experience in store that year and well, I couldn't help it. I didn't plan it exactly, but I could feel that something was going down this year.

The buildup, the weeks of church, music and Rankin Bass specials were the ultimate seasonal flavor of every childhood in my world. The Chipmunks, Bing Crosby and of course, Peanuts. Quoting songs and movies. Classic family moments like opening one present on Christmas Eve, dad reading "The Night Before Christmas" and footie pajamas. Littered with a hint of all night fatigue as we hoped to get a glimpse of Santa.

Some families are organized. They go one by one, they open the gift, read the directions, move from one kid to the next and make it a whole day thing. Not the Russ'. We get shit done. Four weeks of shopping, wrapping and making sure each kid is even and did we get what we like, is over in about seven minutes. Then my mom would sort out who accidently opened whose gifts and make peace with the idea that Santa had a rogue elf that year and can't explain why Brandon got a Barbie instead his sister. In fairness, it was quick because we owned a family business. Timpane's Jewelry store. Started by my Great-Grandfather and handed down over generations. My parents were beyond exhausted. 80-hour work weeks, late nights, odd hours and let's not forget the 1-2 times a week call from Sister Mary Knucklepants. It was their first day off since Thanksgiving, if you can call cooking for twenty a day off.

Natalie woke me up that morning. She was only three years younger than me, and had the anxiety of a Gemini who can't keep a secret. Her 6-year-old excitement set the tone. Dad walked out with his coffee. Mom directed traffic as to where everyone would sit. My sisters were bright eyed and ready to roll. Muppets Christmas Carol playing on the record player as the soundtrack. Everyone was settled.

I turned to my youngest sister, Chandra holding a present waiting for green light, "You're gonna love that Cabbage Patch Doll."

My parents looked at each other in disbelief. Mission 'man up' was a failure with the nine-year-old. The rage in my mom's eyes and the defeat in my dad's, didn't stop me from handing them their presents and saying, "Nice Shoots and Ladders, great slinky, that doll is smaller than your old one," and who can forget, 'This sweater is ugly and mom is going to make you wear it to church."

"FIVE GOLDEN RINGS!" The kids buried my parents disgust with a three-part harmony in the key of miserable.

I blurted out every present before they opened it. As much as I was an asshole, my sisters thought I was a good guesser. It didn't take away from their experience at all. But for my parents, it was the bond that was a thin line between two people trying to make it special, keep it a secret and pull it off at the same time. I was walking across that tightrope with pressure I didn't understand until years later when I became a parent myself. I didn't need to apologize to my sisters. I needed to respect my parents.

Psychometry is a skill I developed more in the years to come, but the first lesson was WHEN to use it. By the end of

John Denver singing "We Wish You a Merry Christmas," it was over.

All in the Family

Another childhood memory was going to Easter at my Aunt Gerrie's house. It was when I realized this was the real family business I needed to go into. My grandmother was always a little ostentatious in her approach, but my Aunt Gerrie, was downright eccentric. We drove down to New Jersey first thing in the morning to Gerrie's modest house. It was decked out in black and white checkerboard EVERYTHING. She had metallic tumblers and giant dice on the floor that I loved.

Then the phone rang. Gerrie stood up and said, "That's Merry and it's a boy." My Uncle Charles picked up the phone and smiled. "Well, you don't say! Merry and Arbie are having a baby!" he shouted to the room.

I saw firsthand how someone could deliver a message and it didn't seem weird to me. I was a bouncy kid in a white leisure suit with a curly mop of hair and blue eyes. I was used to attention. But when my aunt huddled me and my parents around during the goodbyes that day, she took me by my chin and said, "This boy is special. He will lead people in knowing and he will be surrounded by strong people that understand how to change the world." My mom navigated the traditional Connery gathering knowing that the last hour had more alcohol than most 2AM closing calls. I know she took it in stride, but I'll never forget that my Aunt Gerrie looked into my eyes as she said it. Most importantly, she saw me.

She showed me how to deliver a message of encouragement.

The Dull Roar

By the time I got to high school, I realized I needed to find my own way. We moved to live with my grandmother, who had early signs of dementia/Alzheimer's, and were about 20 minutes from everything I knew. No more hanging out in the neighborhood, no more home after the streetlights came on. No more baseball until the sun went down.

I was just far enough away to have to start a new life. I finished the last year of Catholic School in 8th grade living outside the sphere of the neighborhood. But to a 13-year-old kid, it might as well have been Siberia. I was bused in and out to school, on a routine that allowed for no social life. Didn't they know that Aquarius was in my seventh house? I had to get my social on. I died a little between the summer of 8th and 9th grades. I missed so much of 8th grade, nearing the legal limit of absences. I was even sick with something that I over embellished, a la Ferris Bueller. Instead of being non-descript, I went for it as my number of sick days was getting up there. Next thing I knew, I was sitting in a room with people wearing Hazmat suits They were drawing blood and using an ectoplasm reader-type thing on my chest. The machine, without warning, shut off and couldn't be rebooted. Someone didn't want me to be exposed or divulge whatever they were testing me with. This was something that happened often on my path. I was being protected by unseen circumstances. In this case, a likely 'it will be fine' dose of radiation.

I ended up being sent home and put into quarantine with pamphlets on the Ebola virus, Influenza, HIV and MRSA. What a time to be trapped in your basement room. I had about five days of nothingness and had nothing to do. Loneliness has an uncurrent and was a catalyst for me. Something was about to change, a leap, forward or backwards. It will happen in loneliness.

We often get asked the question, "What is your favorite holiday?" Or, "Which year was the best?" Well, Thanksgiving reigned supreme for me, and it was the year in which this story took place. This was prime time for me, laughter and antics ensued. Our challenge from the adults was to "keep it to a dull roar." Our response was, "Sorry if the adults are dull." We had a full 10 round wrestling match on the spare bedroom queen-sized bed. Russell, my cousin and four years my senior, cleared the bed with ease at this point, but we ganged up on him. I was the main event star and commentator as I recorded our matches on the tape recorder. You had to remember to hit the red record and play buttons at the same time. Most of the tapes were filled with short jokes, laughter and screeching, followed by the short straw parent that had to calm us down because we were above the dull roar.

With the adults in the formal dining room, it was showtime at the Brandon Cabaret. Holding the funny for hours on end, there was little I wouldn't do to keep the joke going. With a hint of George Carlin, the challenge was to make everyone laugh above the dull roar. Mission accomplished, as my Aunt Kathy broke into the room to start in with her elevated voice, "What is all the noi..nose... milk coming out... Brandon's nose?" Even the adults broke the rules above the dull roar. It was innocent. It was a childhood memory.

The Christmas before my eighth-grade plague, my Aunt Kathy and Uncle Russ came during the sweet spot before New Year's Eve and I was at the age, where even the cool relatives didn't know what to get me. Like my Great Aunt Gerrie, Kathy saw me. She saw who I was and could appreciate me. Or, she loved that I was such a pain in the ass to her sister. Either way, Kathy and I were connected.

Oh yeah, the sweet spot between Christmas and New Year's. My Aunt and Uncle would have the perfunctory visit sans cousins and head home after dinner. It was the year where my acting chops came in handy. During the presents portion of the day, I opened a book. A book. Nothing short of the pink nightmare footie pajamas in "A Christmas Story." This was ranked number two, a book.

During my quarantine from human contact and international travel, I was beyond bored. I decided to clean my room and what I found was that book. A book. I sat there, opened it and read as if it was a treasure, because it was. "The Artist Way" by Julia Cameron became the primer to unlock my intuition. I always found inspiration in different ways, but this book spoke to me. It was a series of exercises that took you out of your comfort zone. It allowed you to explore and challenge yourself. It was a book written with the tangible activity of committing to yourself. There were activities and dreaming beyond where you were. To a kid like me, misunderstood, struggling to find my path and attempting to find my groove, this book was everything. I learned how I work with creativity, and I began to learn how energy flowed through me. It also showed me how much I worked in a stream of consciousness aside from logical progression and societal structure.

I wrote and did about a dozen exercises. It was writing practice and on top of that, it showed me that being different, had a place in this world. I learned how to journal and let my thoughts flow on to the paper. I began to learn how to take funny (and not so funny) moments in my life and turn them into journal entries and even books.

The Middle

I love family vacations, always have. Growing up, even though we owned a family business, we didn't have much in the way of extras. My bicycles were yard sale specials. My clothes were worn until they were see-through. My mom had the grocery budget that made three meals of leftovers and she made it work. But we didn't go without, ever. Every year we had a 'big' vacation. They were still modest by most standards. There were the years that we went camping in a second-rate pop-up trailer that my dad got when someone could not pay for a class ring. It had rips in the canvas, but it was still the best spot in the camper. Even though you got wet in the rain, it was the only source of air conditioning in the tin roof tinder box.

My parents were the cool parents in the neighborhood. They used to be the chaperones for all the teenagers on the family vacation. Little did Lynn, Suzy, Judy, Patsy, Butchie, Jeff, Dave and Lori know that my parents were setting them up for free babysitting in the future. My Uncle Ken, who was about 20 years younger than my dad, was friends with all of them. I loved that he lived with us for a few years. It was a great time to be a kid around the neighborhood as the other kids were all about 10-15 years older than I was. I was the oldest of three kids, but I was their little brother. The community that was created always made me feel safe and a part of something bigger. That feeling has stayed with me. I crave it in fact. Large groups of people looking out for one another.

We did not always bring the neighborhood kids. As my sisters and I got older, we went as just the family. Maybe my parents did not need babysitting any longer. One year we went to Cape Cod, and it was my first experience feeling how powerful water was to me and how it affected my gift. Being surrounded by the ocean virtually anywhere you go on the Cape, was soothing to me. At 15, I had plenty of experiences connecting with Spirit, but this was a time I became vocal about it. I was enjoying the trip, even the sleeping arrangements. We were in a one-bedroom efficiency that had my parents in the bedroom, my sisters on the pull-out couch and me on the cot in the large room alcove. When you walked out of the apartment, you walked past the row of other efficiencies. They were all filled with other northeasterners away for their family vacations. At the end of the row was the road. To the left was the arcade, a fun zone where my $25 of token money was long since gone. And to the right, was a slight downhill to the ocean. You could smell the sea air as my sister, Natalie and I congregated with the other teens. It was no surprise that on vacation, I wanted to hang out with the cool kids. There were about 10 of us in all, just hanging out and talking about whatever kids in 1988 talked about. I remembered the night before I had such a vivid, lucid dream that I was on cloud nine all day.

Then, for whatever reason, I started telling this group of kids that I had never met before, what their middle names were. "Ezekiel, Jefferson, Rose…"

"Wait, how did you know my middle name?!"

"Yeah, wait, that was my middle name!" said another.

"Claire, McClellan, Joseph, Michael." I kept going as if I was in a déjà vu trance. The names just came out of me. They all confirmed that I did in fact, say their middle names. They all took a step back and started to find reasons to go inside in the late dusk of mid-July. I had two lessons that evening. First, middle names mattered to me. I wasn't sure if it was because there is often a family tie to the middle name, or it had something to do with Brandon being my middle name. If that was how Spirit wanted to connect for me, I needed to accept it and understand it. The second was that I needed to learn context and delivery. I kinda, sorta ruined the social aspect of that vacation. My sister hammered it home when she said, "See what you did? That is why no one hangs out with us! Rein it in…"

What I realized was the importance of my namesake, T. Brandon was my grandfather. He was an optometrist by trade but ran the family jewelry business he inherited. The coincidence of being a Medium (third eye) and owning a crystal shop, had its parallel to an optometrist owning a jewelry store.

Everyone in the city of Cohoes knew Timpane's Jewelers. In the 1950's, everyone knew my grandfather. He was kind and deliberate. He was a poet, a statesman and a volunteer Mountie for the police. He had a love of baseball and started the city little league when he got the other downtown businesses together to pay for uniforms, and nine gloves and a bat. He made sure every kid in the city could see, even if it meant slipping a pair of glasses into their pocket and refusing payment.

Every time I see "Field of Dreams," I think the Moonlight Graham character, was really my grandfather. He gave up other dreams to become what he was meant to be. A theme that showed itself to me over and again. It wasn't just about living the dream; it was about being a realist and knowing what the world needs from you. You *could* play baseball, but you *need* to become a healer and help others. It was one of the hard lessons I learned. Spirit is in charge. The choice is yours. How you manage it, is the soul path you are living.

Buddha Girl

\$2.95 was the going rate for a 'counter' person at Bruegger's Bagels when I was 15 years old. But I took it with the hope for the room for advancement that the shift supervisor sold me on. It was a lie to make sure I worked more shifts than I missed. I actually blossomed because I did advance and it became hard work. By the time I was a senior, I was a Master Baker (we always played with the words on that one) and a supervisor. I was kinda a big deal.

Mind you, that didn't mean that I wasn't down for any shenanigans in spite of my prestige. I did re-write the lyrics to Billy Joel's, "We Didn't Start the Fire" and tailored it to "We Didn't Burn the Onions." And let's not forget the crooner laden remake of the U2 classic, "With or Without Cream Cheese." With the latitude they gave the training staff to 'try new things' and make their products cutting edge, they would have been better served having rules. I kicked open the bake room door on a busy Saturday morning, with a line out the door and dozens of bagels flying off the shelves. I held my new invention over my pony-tailed, painter cap covered head and yelled, "BEHOLD THE GREATEST FOOD STUFF EVER MADE. RESPECT AND WORSHIP ME AS I AM NOW YOUR NEW LEADER!"

I threw the 'Pretzel Deluxe' into the dining room as the manager essentially lost her mind and scolded me back to the bake room, while the entire restaurant and everyone in it burst into confusion and laughter. Yeah, I was *that* guy you worked with in high school. I had great friendships and my gift was just hanging out. I'd pull an all-nighter on a Friday with my best friend Scott playing Nintendo, walk to work or hitch a ride with the police, because they knew I would give them free coffee. I worked the early shift on Saturday, repeated the all-nighter to Sunday, only then to go to church. My tilted halo always needed adjusting. Ya know, I was a regular teenager with Mars in Capricorn.

The employee pool always had a mix of kids from the local college. Siena college was just two miles up the road and when we moved to live with my grandmother, we were across the street from the campus. It was not uncommon for me crash a college party, find street cred with my day job and be accepted as one of their own. When I met Stephanie, it was a chance meeting and the world seemed normal.

Some people have stories about how a woman made them a man. The nervousness about their first time or the one that got away. What Stephanie did was make me human.

She invited me to her dorm room, and we walked all the way back to campus after working together. When we arrived outside Hennepin Hall, there was a stone cross that graced the top of the entrance. as customary for Franciscan Colleges. Behind the cross, was a statue of Buddha. As you walked in, the statue spilled over the sides of the cross. That was her room. Enlightenment awaited.

We ordered a pizza and sat on the floor. The discussion was flush with philosophy, religion and a smattering of hopes and dreams. We dove down rabbit holes about the intention of biblical texts, the virtues of Mary Magdalene and Lilith. We peeled back the Dead Sea Scrolls and the unscrupulous edit of the bible. We went point/counterpoint about female equality, politics and even baseball.

She introduced me to the idea that instead of chasing God, we are God, depending on how we act and our socioeconomic conditioning. Not to mention our own willingness to open and understand our purpose as we evaluate our successes and failures with the sole intention to apply our knowledge to become the best version of ourselves. To make an impact on the world we are the stewards of.

God sent me my intellectual equal to teach me.

The verbal sparring was that of gladiators in the great Colosseum. Her Aquarius breath and vision for the world was on a green sheet of her astrological chart in front of me. "Leo Rising" she pointed to her first house. "Oh my moon, the phases, do you know what your moon is? I'm Aquarius right here in the 7th house, next to Venus and Pluto and of course my sun. It tells me so much."

Stephanie talked a language I could hardly understand. But I was fascinated. She could have just as easily pulled out a periodic table and told me about how she was going to find a cure for the common cold with nuclear fusion and a pinch of Mendelevium. I was hooked with how she spoke, the depth of her knowledge and the design of her intention.

Then somewhere in the night, when we finished the coldest slice of pizza and the last swallow of strawberry wine, I told her that she made me feel less broken. I was confessing how I was really struggling with the roles in life, the expectations and my perception of being different. Dead people, they talk, I hear them. I used to think they were imaginary people that were showing me how to be creative or funny. Turns out they were dead, all of them. She was empathetic and without judgement. "I know spirit flows through you; you are a healer."

Then the flood gates opened.

Toad the Wet Sprocket came through in the distance.

"She said, "I'm fine, I'm okay"

Cover up your trembling hands

There's indecision when you know you ain't got nothing left"

She looked at me, then away, then again deep into me. "I'm not broken," she said. The tears flowed like a dam break. I watched her release. She confessed the deepest of wounds that I promised to never repeat. She ebbed through sorrow, pain and anger.

"When the good times never stay

And the cheap thrills always seem to fade away

When will we fall?

When will we fall down?"

The things she said, were things I was conditioned to judge. I was quiet. Like a mighty oak. Say nothing, just be. I absorbed everything she said, I could feel her. Spirit showed me the details she left out, the emotion of a past that should have been prosecuted. She just needed my shoulder, with her eyes shut tight she was willing to believe in any brand of God to make sure this pain went away. All I could do was absorb.

"She hates her life, she hates her skin

She even hates her friends

Tries to hold on to all the reputations she can't mend

And there's some chance we could fail

But the last time, someone's always there for bail"

She looked up at me with the bags packed for vacation under her eyes and thanked me.

"You want to run, don't you. I understand. I'm horrible." I sat there frozen. I showed how responsible I am by having a job, I had ok grades and was super active in church. But this was the first time I felt like I made an adult decision. I HAD to break my conditioning for this soul.

I reassured her and held her tight.

When her roommate came in drunk from a last hurrah, she smattered a couple of curses and congratulated us both on getting lucky. She fell into her bed fully clothed. Steph looked at me and said, "Do you want to see something really healing?" She said it in a mysterious but captivating tone. You would sign up for anything, even if it involved running over a train bridge and finding a dead body.

She gave me one of her flannels as she slipped one on herself. We ran down the stairs and out into pre-dawn chill of early May. We walked down a side road and slid between a rancher fence and out across the field. As we approached the barn, she held her finger up to her lips and hushed me. She pushed against a ragged door and was careful not to clamor the gate attached.

Stephanie walked with her hands outreached to the stall. That's where his nose came out of the darkness. In a familiar greeting, she buried her head into his neck. He responded with a gentle push back. The dim light caught Stephanie's long blond hair that nearly reached her waist. Her pear-shaped hourglass figure was undeniably full, but graceful in every moment connected with our new adventure. In that moment, I truly saw her. I saw her as human.

She took my hand and walked me into the stall. "Like this," she said as she put my hands on his heart. "This is Arete and he's my healer." We stood in the stall on either side of that beautiful horse who knew his purpose and had no desire to be any more of less than the conduit of a connection in that moment.

We stood there for what seemed like forever. I couldn't see Stephanie around Arete, but I could feel her. I could feel the earth. I could feel the rhythm of the earth through this gentle beast. All of the pain we just exchanged went into him and into the ground.

We heard the door to the adjacent farmhouse open. I looked around Arete's head and she said, "Hide!"

WHAT!? My brain was going a mile a minute. The buzz had long since passed and now I was fighting my circadian rhythm to stay upright and think clearly. We buried under a blanket in the back of the stall. I looked at her in disbelief as well as amazement. "We're in trouble, aren't we?" She just held her finger to her lips. We heard whoever it was go back inside as if they forgot their keys and that's when we escaped. As we left the stall, Arete nodded to her as she stroked his nose one more time. We ran across fields, behind houses and found ourselves on the back end of a country club where we sat and watched the sun rise.

We laughed hard about our adventure. Our night. Our lifetime. We spent the last 18 hours together and weren't bored. Our brains were engaged, we found trouble, healing and connection. As the daylight broke, she explained that Arete was not a real creature in Greek philosophy, but rather the idea of becoming. The idea of finding your greatest potential and never being compromised. Having an irrevocable moral compass that was self-evident. We debated the philosophy about the "Sun of God" and the Rise on the third day and the 12 Apostles. Were the Zodiac around the sun and... and...   God sent me my intellectual equal as the Sun came up over the valley below. But nothing thrives in the dark. Light shows the truth.

After our walk of shame across the back nine to her dorm, the fatal blow came that had to show me that life is a series of moments, and nothing will ever last.

"So, what are you going to do after graduation?"

"I'm thinking about Siena," I replied.

The puzzled and shocked look on her face is something that will never leave me.

"Wait, you're in high school?"

She shook her head slowly. "No. Please no. I thought you were a Theology major." Both our vulnerabilities spilled back into us. "I'm taking off, you're just beginning. I can't." The reality of a 4.0 Psychology student weeks away from graduation with her acceptance to post grad Duke meets the kid with community college back up all locked in, hit her. She turned and walked into her dorm without me. I looked up at her window. The cross. The Buddha. The light came on and I turned and walked home. I was at least the guy that made sure she got home safely.

I never saw her again. But If I ever get a chance, I will tell her how inspirational that moment was. I wouldn't be the person I am today without it. There were so many tentacles of what my life would become that began that night. It would be easy to call her the one that got away and that could be true, but there was nothing romantic about our time together. She was a teacher. She showed me knowledge I needed. I was a safe place. A place for her to give her confessions and never be reminded of them again.

Bombardier to Pilot, Come In

Cape Cod was a catalyst for me again years later. I was vacationing with my wife, sister and brother-in-law, and their two daughters. I woke up one day feeling anxious. It's not an uncommon feeling to be stimulated by the emotions or energy around me, but this was something different. During the week-long vacation, it was the worst weather day of the week. Which means...shopping, I guess. My enjoyment on the Cape was watching the summer baseball league and eating lobster rolls and ice cream like a connoisseur. So, a full day of visiting Christmas Tree shops and the same T-Shirt chain in every hamlet on the Cape, had its draw backs. Plus, I felt ANXIOUS.

The only way that I could describe how I felt was an unending pressure against me from an unseen force, like time or youth slipping away. I wasn't sure what the source was, but I can tell you, I was restless and irritable the entire day. I was like Clark W. Griswold at that Grand Canyon, everywhere we went. Two minutes of sightseeing and I knew it wasn't going to get much better. I needed to keep moving. I was rushing between each location like I had someplace to be. I didn't enjoy lunch or even my sixth lobster roll of the vacation. The company I was with was also not enjoying my antics. I didn't mean it, but I couldn't help it. It was almost like having an anxiety disorder without the diagnosis. I was a little worried.

"I want to get ice cream," I blurted out like some sort of vacation Tourette's.

"Sure," my wife said. "So long as it's near an ocean so we can push you in after today. What the hell is wrong with you?"

I guess it was evident that my anxiousness was taking away from the day.

We had a favorite spot we had already hit up three times by mid-week. Their homemade peanut butter cup ice cream was the best on Route 28. We stood in the long line, knowing the ice cream was worth it. Then I felt like I was hit by an 18-wheeler. I felt time slow down and all my senses were on overload. I stood with my family, but I was more distant than ever.

I could smell burning oil. The kind that comes from combustion engines. I could hear a loud engine and felt vibration all around me. I saw a tall man with a bomber jacket and a leather flight cap with padding around the ears. I heard the shouting and the rumble. Then the gun smoke smell was up deep into my nostrils. He was working back and forth from one side of the tin tube to the other. He kept opening crates and dropping nine yards down into a pit where the gun smoke rose.

He stopped what he was doing and turned to look at me.

"Tell them he's going to be OKAY! I've got him, like I've got this ship. I've got my boy!" He grabbed the bottom of his leather bomber jacket and straightened it with a snap motion to make sure I saw it.

Then an explosion came up from the shaft as this tall shadowy man dove in and grabbed the gunner with both arms. The smoke was thick and I started to cough hard.

"Are you alright?" my six-year-old niece asked me. Everyone looked at me like I had just mooned a school bus.

"I'm fine," I said clearing my throat.

I looked ahead in the line as I regained my composure. I was still in my déjà vu-dream feel when a woman seemed to stand out and everyone else became shadowed around her. It was clear what I had just experienced had something to do with her. I jumped the line and walked up to her.

"Excuse me," I said. She turned and looked up at me with sad eyes. "I don't mean to interrupt you and I know this might sound crazy." When someone says, 'this might sound crazy,' you know that main course crazy is about to be served.

"I'll buy you an ice cream if I'm wrong. But, I'm a Medium and I sense a tall thin man in the back of a World War II gunner ship. He's helping the gunners and even saved someone from the pit? He said Christopher to me twice." I saw her face run through the range of emotions from crazy, validation, fear, shock and then relief. She put the pieces together of what I just told her.

She looked at me and said, "I'm not sure what you are really saying or why you would really know any of that." I stood there digging my hand into my pocket, ready to give her $20 for ice cream. "That was my father. He was a gun runner in the back of a B-52 during the air raids over Germany. He made over 50 runs and was shot down twice. He saved a gunner that got hit and almost fell through and out into the night."

I stood there in awe. First because of the willingness she had to give me validation. Second because I freaking got it right! "There's more," I said.

"He said, 'he's going to be okay, I have him' and fixed his jacket and dove to save the gunner."

She stood there shocked as the line moved forward around us. Her husband had his mouth open and she began to cry and said, "I knew it."

I was bewildered and begged for some explanation. Her husband hugged her while she released the tension that I read on her earlier. As she gained her composure, she took my hand and said, "Thank You."

"We dropped my son off at Otis Air Force Base this morning. He is headed to active duty and I asked my father to watch over him, no in fact, I begged him to watch over him. That is why we named him after my father, William Christopher."

I had real validation. I had deep impact and was beginning to learn that messages don't need to be lifesaving or even profound, but rather, timely. They ended up buying our ice cream instead, which was totally unnecessary, but I did expect it as I ordered the triple peanut butter cup.

We talked a little bit longer as we ate our ice cream and she shared what a proud soldier her son was and how proud they are as parents. She grew up in a military family and purposely didn't marry a military man. Only to have her son have a passion for aviation and talked about being in the Air Force since he was five. I simply said, "You named him for his journey."

As we parted, we exchanged pleasantries, even hugs. She asked, "Would you like to see something before you go?"

"Sure," I said following her and her husband to their car.

"My son wore it all the way there today. It's our family's keepsake and our most honored heirloom." Her husband opened the trunk where her father's bomber jacket laid in plastic.

Pay Attention

I had been taking Psychic Development classes for about two years and I wasn't sure what I was doing yet. I think I was in the same groove most people are in when they take classes like those for a while. You get into a rut of trying to pay attention to EVERYTHING and finding meaning in EVERYTHING. Wait, I noticed the man who said 'hello' to me was wearing green, so that must mean heart Chakra and healing energy. My order number was 14, which reduces to five and means change, so I have change coming. And I kept hearing the same phrase over and again, so when I heard someone actually say, "Yo, what's up," my mind would race to understand. Overload and fatigue. It would happen when you experienced an 'awakening' and you needed to take a break from it. You know, go back to the 'old way' of eating take out, listening to nonsense music and having mindless fun.

I was in one of those ruts when I learned a valuable lesson. Never ignore messages because I am meant to deliver them to the people who need them.

Sitting in the parking lot of the Albany Jewish Community Center, I was almost an hour early for the co-ed softball showdown between the Convicts and the Neon Knights. The Convicts wore roadside safety orange because it was the cheapest shirt, and the Knights wore neon yellow shirts that glowed even after the sun went down. They were led by Dick Davert, the owner of the company sponsor. He owned a cleaning business and in a co-ed beer league, he had the hottest commodity, women that could play. In the last game, they drubbed us and told us to pour beer on our 29-3 loss. They were ruthless.

Our team consisted of 22 players, of which only three filled the co-ed requirement. We needed four to start a game, or lose an out every time we came to bat. We were often looking for one more female player at every game and never thought to ask them, "Can you actually play softball?"

But that didn't matter to the rag tag team that we were. There were often 12 guys on the bench, drinking beer, talking about wrestling and Metallica. If you were lucky, you got one at bat and played a little in the field. Even though I was batting over .700 I rarely saw the field, didn't drink beer and basically couldn't stand wrestling. It was a wonder I would show up at all.

Then I remembered why I signed up to play in the first place. I was trying to lose weight and being active in as many ways as possible. Even though I didn't play much, there was still practice and forcing myself to put on sneakers. I would take a few trips around the outside of the field to be active. That was the important part, I was active. I was going to the gym a couple times a week and playing softball with a three game a week schedule. I weighed over 420 pounds when I started to lose weight. I had already lost over 50 pounds by changing my diet and joining this ridiculous beer league. If there was one thing I was determined to be, it was consistent.

That's why on a beautifully sunny late June evening, I was sitting in my car and dreading playing. I was forcing myself to go. Every fiber of my body was telling me NOT to play. I thought

I had reached the fatigue of losing weight. I had spent a lot of time reading about the mental game of weight loss. Every article talked about the pitfalls of what gets you off track. This was a major red flag. Fatigue.

Using my flip phone, I sent a text to my wife. About ten texts actually. "Is the sink leaking?" "How tall is the grass?" "Are the Christmas lights still up?"

She simply responded, "Nope."

I remember walking down the hill and meeting the others on the first base side. It was that perfect evening where you didn't care if you played or not. It was the perfect temperature, with the perfect breeze and the perfect coolness of the grass. I sat there and watched the team play five innings of one run softball. Our team wasn't 'hitting it where they ain't'. However, on the field we were just as atrocious. Our team allowed 19 runs in just over an hour. We accidentally scored somewhere along the way or we would have forfeited by the fourth inning. That's when our manager was like screw it, send in the scrubs and I got my chance to bat.

Sitting on the summer grass and taking power naps in between errors, makes you a little rusty. So, I stretched out and took my $100 bat up to the plate. Before I tell you the rest of the story, I have to brag that back in the day, I was quite a ball player. I played until I was 19 and even played semi-pro for a couple of games. Then one day, I couldn't catch up to a fast ball. It happens to nearly every kid that has dreams of becoming Kirby Puckett.

As you can imagine, I had stars in my eyes knowing I was going to see a meatball right over the plate. And there it was, right over the middle of the plate. I kept my eyes locked and my bat steady. What happened next can only be described as the shot heard round the world. However, it wasn't the crack of the bat, as the titanium alloy showed no mercy as it crushed the yellow leather ball sending it toward the Ben Shalom wing almost a quarter mile away. Everyone cheered as I heard, "That's out of here!" and "Oh man, no more bench for B!!"

I did something you should never do. I watched the ball sail between two outfielders, who were playing deep to start. The ball carried and I looked to see the other base runner score with ease. That's when we heard it.

I rounded first base and was halfway to second, when we heard what we thought was a gunshot. I happened to see the cheering sideline duck when they heard it. BOOM! Next thing I know I'm on the ground like a sack of hammers and I can't move my leg. I felt the adrenaline and shock overcome my body as I laid in the cool dirt. True to form Dick Davert, the star second baseman, tagged me out to end the game as he asked me if I was ok.

I retraced what occurred by talking to various people that were there. Apparently, I caught my cleat on first base causing my Achilles to rupture. It took a week to have an emergency surgery and I didn't walk on my own two feet for almost six months. I was confined to a lazy boy most of the time and that's when I started paying attention to what happened.

It was my left leg, my intuitive side. The left side is also the feminine side. I was clearly not listening as my alpha male ears told me I needed to play that game. I was put in an energetic time out to be told, "If you're not going to listen, we need to make the message stronger." My lesson was listening, trusting and honoring what I was getting. There was no reason for me to play that day. I needed to work on my feminine side.

I realized, I needed to pay attention. Spirit was subtle with the signs, even when it was in my face when I wasn't listening.

The Duality of Buddy Christ

Being born and raised Catholic puts you in the front row of many things. My entire life, I watched my family become stewards of a community before Sunday kick-off. My volunteerism brought me to be an Alter boy, Eucharistic minister, lecturer, choirboy, usher and eventually a teacher. I took solace in seeing people be real, let down their hair and be human. Before the age of 18, I was part of the 'inside' of a Catholic Church parish and was teaching and guiding Confirmation candidates on their decisions for adulthood.

What a coup! A long haired, hip, young, educated servant to the cause. It would be great for recruitment and street cred. What I saw and heard after the regular classes, retreat planning and post mass gossip, had me questioning everything that was said. Whether in the pulpit, in Sunday School or in 'Religion' classes, which were designed to teach the information properly. I began to realize it was an indoctrination process.

The incident that sent me over the edge was that of legend and was for the most part, completely unnecessary. When working with Confirmation candidates, we were asking kids to become adults, then expecting them to move from, "being seen but not heard" to regurgitating righteous indignations. As much as the dialogue was about the maturing process, it showed itself as a false flag for all to see.

Jill was a good kid. She attended church every week, turned her work in on time, went to Catholic school and was ready to volunteer at a moment's notice. It turned out, she also had hormones. Jill had set her eyes on Danny, a favorite of the resident priest. The priest was close to his family, had dinner with them regularly and even vacationed with them once or twice. Danny was also a good kid. He volunteered at the drop of a hat and held many of the same roles I did. Only he had real potential to become a priest, and openly talked about it.

When Jill put the press on Danny to do more than hold hands, the confessional exploded. The resident priest took the confidentiality of a confession and turned it into a three-ring circus. He held an emergency meeting with all the teachers and proceeded to berate each of us for encouraging their relationship, even though none of us knew anything about it. He brought Jill in after class and made her sit across the room from the four of us on the teaching committee.

That's where he slut shamed her for almost an hour. He wasn't kind, he wasn't God Fearing, he was mean. He was angry and I was not at all impressed with the way he was handling it. When I spoke up in her defense, or to at least give an attempt for her to have some breathing room, he warned me I was next in the seat, and if I wanted to join her I could. What I was most upset about, was this was an opportunity to coach her and use real life examples about consequence, communication and faith-based decision making. Instead, this steam roller had only one agenda. Decades of volunteerism dismissed in a matter of moments.

I understood right then, fascist authoritarians can't be challenged. You need to change them by changing their surroundings. He was willing to sacrifice a girl on her path for his own agenda and to shame her, in order to work out his own fears and promises to the diocese. I decided to work on an educational platform beyond words.

Confirmation is known as the 'big lie.' You lie to your sponsor, who lies to the bishop, who lies to God, who knows the truth anyway about how you are being forced into a dog and pony show. A show that is complicit about taking on the responsibility of being an adult in the church. How do we change that? Ummm, using the actual truth. I spent days re-writing the final two lessons for Confirmation.

Instead of it being an indoctrination, it was an exercise of knowledge and applied values. Each student did research on a different World View or Sect of Christianity and did a comparison against Catholicism. Really progressive stuff and George Carlin would have been proud. Imagine the feedback from parents commenting on how healthy it was that their son did a comprehensive deep dive on the comparison of Buddha and Jesus, and how the beliefs were similar and different. Or the parent who thanked the program for acknowledging that the riff in their family between the Catholic side and the Episcopal side had only one major difference, and it opened a dialogue with the family.

I received that feedback not as a thank you, but rather a series of questions and an ultimate dismissal from the post class meeting. I knew I was in trouble, but I didn't know how much. I was in trouble for teaching adults how to discern what they believe in, not by staying ignorant, but by making a conscious decision.

The phone rang shortly after 11 pm that night. It was the bishop. Not the local priest, not the education director, the freaking bishop.

"Brandon, it is Reginald." I had only met him a few times, but his voice was instantly recognizable.

"Oh, um, hi. What's going on?"

"Did you teach the tenants of Buddhism tonight to one of *my* Confirmation classes?"

"Yes, sure did. I also explained the pillars of Islam, the tradition of the Satyr and why the Church of England has a red door."

"I see." He was doing a damage assessment and it was much worse than he thought.

"Your services are no longer required. You are not to speak to anyone about this and you are not to attend mass or teach classes until you appeal this decision to the Diocesan Council for reinstatement."

Cancel culture 1993 style. My mom was devastated. My dad wasn't sure what to say.

I stopped going to church regularly. When I did attend it was to other parishes. I explored other walks of faith and in the end, realized that the Bishop had done me a favor. The Catholic Church didn't serve my needs and I was tired of constantly chasing approval. And just like that, it was gone.

I was a free agent. Free to explore the world, my beliefs and free to help whomever I damn well pleased.

Years later, I needed to finish a bachelor's degree. I found one of those fancy cohort schools that was geared toward real life. Credits were earned for time served in the working world and they became essays about life lessons and building applied knowledge. I inadvertently attended a Mission College with a strong religious ministry. I was hooked because I could get my degree in a matter of a year or so, but not once did they say I would need to take religious studies to accompany my organizational management core. Fine print and Pisces don't go together. But here we go.

In one of the core sessions, we would have guest teachers who specialized in their subject. My primary was a wonderful woman, who was rooted in her faith and could speak eloquently about problem solving from an ethical compass. She didn't judge anyone outwardly and had been a corporate leader for years before I met her. She had a way of teaching the school's agenda without being indoctrinating to a Christian diatribe and encouraged each of us to find our style and voice. She was an incredible cheerleader and compass. My degree thesis was an evaluation of the Catholic Church as a business. I used key phrases such as strained resources (priests), diminished demand (attendance) and consolidation of operations (church closures). I took faith, scandal and soul saving out of the equation and let it stand on its merits as a product. I predicted mass closings, a brief resurgence and an ultimate niche following that served the elite instead of the poor.

When it came to "World Views" class, having an evangelical preacher teach the core session could only end badly for me. His idea of world view was to clearly acknowledge that there are other ideas, cultures and ways of life, but make no mistake, they were wrong. Jesus Christ was the only way in or out of not only heaven, but this class credit. Reverend Jim also had a side hustle to bring God to everyone. He was the proprietor of a YouTube channel that promoted his weekly sermons and we would hear about the number of views and 'likes' he had, as if he was talking about the football game statistics from last Sunday.

The final paper was a comparison of the three major world views and to make a clear-cut argument for which you believe in. What he was looking for from us, was to trash Islam for its violence, Judaism for its arcane tradition and Buddhism for its spiritual nonsense. I crafted a well-tailored masterpiece that cited the superiority of Christianity by way of the staying power of the Gospel, the number of followers worldwide by weight of comparison, the presence of the validation of the Dead Sea Scrolls and of course, the trueness of God's intention.

Remember the scene in the movie "A Christmas Story," when Ralphie hands his teacher his paper on wanting a Red Ryder BB Gun and she found it to be the masterpiece she had longed for her entire teaching career? A+++++++++.

"Brandon, Reverend Jim. This is amazing work. I'm truly impressed with your paper. There is someone I would like meet."

I was being invited to meet another pastor who had a mega church down south and was interested in coming to the Capital District. We met at a 70's style Italian restaurant with a curved booth and tuxedo-clad waiters.

"You really are a servant of the Lord, aren't you? Jim told me you know the bible and have a gift of the gab to encourage and enlighten." His southern accent, phosphorescent teeth and winks, told me all I needed to know about what was going down here.

I sat in the center of the curved booth. His two minions sat on either side of me and Buddy Christ sat across from me. They ordered hard drinks, expensive meals and added on whatever looked good on the menu. I drank water and got the Chicken Parm.

"Jesus told me that you would walk into my life. I knew my faith would pay off," he said with a giddiness that stole the mood. "What's your favorite passage to inspire people?"

We bantered back and forth pulling from the books of Ezekiel, Daniel, Isaiah and Psalms.

My years of memorization were solid. My delivery was convincing enough to have his henchmen chime in at the end of the passage, "Amen!" That's when the tone turned.

"Son, how much money do you want to make?" He motioned to the waitress, "Honey, another one of these, make it two." He held up his empty glass of bourbon and pointed to it.

"I never thought much of making money for being a steward of faith." I explained that being a corporate recruiter had set me up just fine in the world.

"Oh, come on now, everyone wants something bigger. Bigger house, deeper pool, fancier car. Take that car you drove in here with. How about something, say from this year?" I sat there stymied as he babbled on about how the depth of the Lord's abundance would give me all I needed as he shot back one bourbon, and high classed the next with a sip or two. The minions followed suit and praised Jesus, called him by name and said Amen!

The car I was driving was my mother-in-law's. The one my mentor knew that her clothes were still in the trunk.

"I see great things in you, but only if you step up to the podium and take what is yours. These sheep want to be lead. They want to be told the way to the Kingdom. They want it to come from you and I will share with you all the abundance that the Lord has promised me and promised you. Spirit came to me and told me you are MY Chosen one." His sermon of Brandon caught the attention of the room. His words were offset by clumsy actions, excited undertones and the intention of closing the deal.

I cleared my throat, "I'm sorry, I'm not for sale."

The laughter stopped and he leaned in. He rested his gold bracelet on the table and reached up to his crucifix around his neck to stroke it. "Are you saying Jesus is a liar to me?"

"This reminds me of what Peter said about pride. He knew something about it because he denied what believed in and regretted it. So, I take precedence when his words have made it this far through time and into my mind to remember it and to speak it." I then quoted,

"Be alert and of sober mind. Your enemy the devil prowls around like a roaring lion looking for someone to devour. Resist him, standing firm in the faith, because you know that the family of believers throughout the world is undergoing the same kind of sufferings."

I was talking about lost lightworkers that only had 'Religion' as a means to explore what they believed in. He thought I was talking about bourbon and the weak. I was standing in my truth and nowhere else.

I thanked him for the meal, the time and the education. That night, I re-wrote the paper I sent to Reverend Jim. It was vastly different, as I cited the wholesale theft of the bible from Gilgamesh (Noah) to Beatitudes and the Buddhist way of life. I cited how ignorance and peer pressure grew a faith that was not strong enough to survive, because the purpose of a great Master like Jesus was to do things in JOY of life, not in fear of damnation. The message was changed in 400AD by Constantine and further bastardized by clever edits from John Smith and King James. They slanted the perception and wrote most eloquently about the difference between a person's "Truth" and THE Truth.

I thanked him for his time to read the paper and the education. Both pastors are very professional and know their game well. They are respected by their congregations, so who was I to get in the way of that. I learned that I needed to understand my faith and what it meant to ME. I understood Faith was an inside job because humans will always get it wrong.

The Stream of Consciousness

I was trying to figure out how I worked, what made me tick. I didn't understand how much I was flying in the dark, until I saw my first professional Medium's show. At this point, I had performed over 20 live events. The arena sat 1,800 people, and this well-known international Medium, read nine people and closed out with a Celine Dion showstopper. She dedicated the song to all the deceased in the room. She had a lovely singing voice, hit the comparable notes and gracefully left the stage to end her time. I realized a few things.

First, I had been performing live shows for nearly two years without ever taking notes from other Mediums. I was trying to be my own person. But it was the equivalent of being in a band but never seeing a live concert. Second, I watched her technique. I saw the pattern in which she would receive energy and messages. The conversation that flowed from it and the reaction of the few people she connected with. Lastly, I saw the combination of modalities. Her need to go full artist with her closing, gave me hope to sing "Silent Lucidity" at the end of every event. However, I had a hard time reconciling not connecting with the other 1,791 audience members. It seems like grandstanding a bit when everyone was grieving, so here's a song. I looked at my ticket as a $69.50 lesson with service charges.

All due respect to all of us in this industry. The show was a lot of bullshit. I'm not dismissing her ability, I think and *KNOW* that she was fully connected to spirit and delivering messages.

But the misdirect wasn't healing. People were promised a product and a chance to be with someone they had lost. I simply watched a very gifted person receive just enough validation for her conscious to say, "Good night, Albany!"

Meanwhile, I was hosting shows with 20-40 people several times a month, and I was reading every single person. Plus, the ticket price was nowhere near $70. Granted, I was in training mode and the more experience I got, the better I was for it. I'm sure most Mediums receive proper training techniques. I had been scolded and chastised for reading everyone. I was also criticized for asking a question and making it a dialogue. Although I understood the need for authenticity and integrity, telling me I'm not worthy because you "never feed a Medium" is an arrogant dialogue of just spewing unconfirmed statements that never need to be validated. Truth is, that may have worked for other Mediums, but not for me. I also watched these critical Mediums absolutely bomb readings by not presenting anything connective, let alone evidential.

Being evidential in a reading is everything to a Medium. That is where you present irrefutable evidence that it is a specific Spirit you are connecting with. It is the moment where the sitter will say, "There is no way they would know that." A song, a situation or a sign. There are so many ways. My favorite is when a phrase comes out; hence "Funny You Should Say That!" But there was more to it than just having ah-ha moments and validation from skeptics.

I started to study individual Mediums and how they learned and delivered. I took classes from many of them, even after I had been teaching Intuitive Development for years. I watched how they were committed to a diatribe. One that made you part of a cult, directed to do this and not do that. I also noticed that the vast majority of Mediums fit into two primary categories. Middle-aged housewives that had ample time to develop and gay men. I'm not diminishing their ability at all. I'm simply pointing out that there were very few natural role models for me to learn from. I will vouch for anyone that does this work. It's difficult and you have to find purpose in your delivery and who you are meant to help. And there's an under culture of cattiness, back biting and viciousness.

I decided to visit Lily Dale in upstate NY. Lily Dale is "the place where no one dies" because it's the summer home of resident Mediums. You can find an HBO Documentary on the village. Visitors from all over would come and have two or three readings a day to connect with their loved ones. I went there to find my voice, see how others did it and what I could glean. I went there on a weekend when they had Tibetan Monks in for healing ceremonies. They didn't speak English but communicated by motion and smiles. I sat at a picnic table for the welcome meal at the opening ceremony. On one side of me sat a monk, on the other, a resident Medium. The resident Medium was complaining about the Community Board of Directors, other mediums and then delivered their own showstopper. "All men are scum and I could write a book about everyone's secrets and really turn their worlds upside down." I was sitting between that and a Monk who was grateful that I had an extra napkin. I sat in silence and conveyed smiles of gratitude instead of hearing about rumors of Greenwich Village.

I was dejected to see the lack of humanity from someone on a spiritual path. Later in the weekend, I was walking across the main courtyard when a woman made a bee line for me. "Excuse me…. Excuse me, I see you there. Spirit is near."

She introduced herself as one of the Board members. I held back telling her about the jack wagon Medium I had encountered, as I realized there was more to her redirecting her path to talk to me.

"Your aura is so green, so blue, so yellow. You are new at this, but you are a powerful one."

I smiled and nodded taking a page from the amazing healing ceremony I just attended.

"You aren't like the others, you have to do this alone in many ways, a new path. You have your own voice. As much as I enjoy you as a visitor, don't pick up any of the bad habits of the human side of some of our Mediums." She spoke to the point and cleared up my interaction from the night before. She invited me to speak at the Inspiration Stump. In 1879, this is where platform Mediumship was born. I was offered to do a reading or two because she valued what I had to say. She kept saying to me, "This is important to you, very important."

I watched the first Medium deliver a great general reading based in imagination, while the sitter received no validation and was too kind to say they were wrong. I was offered to go up to the stump next. I proceeded to read all 18 people there. I gave evidence, specifics and kept right on going. I even read the person who was too kind to say she had received a crappy reading.

"What I'm getting is your grandmother, Phyllis. She gives me the buttons, the sewing kit and your Raggedy Anne doll that she kept putting back together." Validation through tears and applause, at a sacred space. The Board member couldn't get word to me that proper etiquette was to read no more than three people, let alone take up an hour.

I was approached afterward to ask how to book me, which house was mine in town and what was my website. I handed out what business cards I had and received the evil eye from my Board member. I'm not sure if she was more upset that I was up there as long as I was, upstaged a resident medium or handed out more cards than anyone else that day. "You are unique, but you need to find yourself."

I then understood that I was looking for influence in all the wrong places.

I went back to what I knew best. I started watching Comedy and listened to Eddie Murphy, George Carlin and Johnny Carson. That's when I realized, I didn't work like other Mediums because I was nowhere NEAR what other mediums were. Instead of looking to John Edwards, James Van Praagh or Lisa Williams, I needed to be looking at Robin Williams.

I began to read every article interview, watched every special, caught every personal appearance and analyzed every movie. Over time, I learned the art of what Robin did. He would prepare with a plan, had specific jokes, knew the ebb and flow from start to finish, and the highs and lows from excitement to poignancies. But when he hit the stage, all bets were off. He was an improv genius. His movie scripts were "written with him in mind," but he performed in the flow of energy at that moment. He wasn't just a genius, he was a conduit. Like Tesla and Nostradamus, he was a conduit of energy. That is what spoke to me.

Robin taught me everything I needed to know about using my gift. He showed me that the power of laughter was far greater than the power of fear. Just as in the movie, "Monsters, Inc." He showed that you have to embrace the ride. The ups, the downs, the mistakes and the joy. "We are only given a spark, we mustn't lose it." He taught me regeneration and showed me how energy flowed from the crowd to Spirit for inspiration and connection. He fed off the other actors, the audience and the rush. Robin was a shining example of a stream of consciousness.

He also taught me the caution to not chase those rushes. There is nothing pleasurable about being inorganic for the laugh or the applause. He showed me that he was human and whole. Robin Williams illustrated the duality of having a gift you are trying to bring to the world and it is important. Our unique blend of talents and experiences help us through and its awkward figuring it out. You will be misunderstood; you will be criticized and you will be judged. You will be a target and you will be derailed. But your gift is the most important thing.

Robin Williams died on August 11th, 2014. An 8 in numerology. He was ready for something new. He was 63 years old, a 9 in numerology. He had done everything he thought he would. You can make the argument that suicide is selfish and a coward's way out. However, his body WAS the magic. He was built to be a conduit and an improvisational genius. His body was betraying him. He had a been diagnosed with Lewey Body Dementia. A progressive disease that slows the synapses in your brain until you can no longer think or act quickly. His body took away his magic. I understood why he wanted to escape.

I heard of his death when it came across my phone and I couldn't speak. I just cried quietly because, I knew what happened and why. I was at a car show and was grabbing an ice cream. I was instantly numb. I wanted to tell him how he impacted me and made me who I was, by simply observing him. I tried to regain myself and continued on. I heard a couple talking about the news, everyone was mentioning it. "It's such a tragedy, they are talking about it as a suicide." A young couple talked about someone they had never met before. I stopped and politely corrected them.

"He didn't kill himself, he went to go see about a girl."

Money Maker Development

What a time to be alive and in my early 30's. Married, house, a 'successful' career. In the early 2000's, it meant only one thing in my social network. Poker night. Every week, sometimes several times a week. The poker boom was real in suburbia. We all loved to tell the story about the time that, "I was sitting there with the nuts and all I could do is watch this guy go fishing and try and bully. But I played it cool and yelled, seat open on table three as I turned my cards over. Busted!". Yeah, us suits by day loved the dramatic.

It was becoming more than hobby for me. I was starting to play weekly and I saw the stakes beginning to rise. I was getting *really* good at playing poker. There was a big difference between a $20 home game with cousins and friends, and a $200 buy in with pit bosses and color ups. I noticed I was combining my passion for the felt with my intuitive ability. I would take a day off every now and again and head to a casino for a tournament. Partly because it was the way I destressed. After all, casinos had buffets. So, if I lost, I would hit up the buffet and head home.

I would hone my intuition into what was going on at the table. I began to read the other player's emotions, fear, excitement and bluffs. I used my intuition with the cards. I announced cards as they were turned over with alarming accuracy. I started to notice which situations I thrived in. For instance, if I was at a blackjack table, I would spend about an hour and quadruple my money. No offense to the very nice blackjack dealers over the years, but they weren't really part of the equation. They were turning the cards over for the 'house'. The lifeless corporation that won't put up clocks or build windows and gave ten cents to the hundred dollars lost in comps. Yeah, I had no problem cleaning up against the man. Doubling on 12, staying at 14, hitting on 17. I didn't do anything by the book, it was all intuition. The energy of the table participants mattered, but my actions were completely me against the man.

However, at the poker table, it was completely different.

Yes, I could sense and feel things. I couldn't 'see' the cards, but I knew if I had them beat and vice versa. It was a typical day for me visiting the casino. I sat at the blackjack table and padded my bankroll for the first hour. I had signed up for a tournament that eventually didn't have enough people to start. That was the universe giving me the high sign. I should have known right then I had a lesson coming.

I had several rush and lull cycles for a few hours while playing a cash game. Rush is when you get the cards to play and lulls are when it is easy to fold the not-good hands. But I promise I won't make this sound like a poker story. The table was full most of the time, with a few of the players there as long as I was. The banter was friendly and with experienced players, the pots were mostly modest. I was up about $1,000. Then the monster hand that we all look for during a full day of poker arrived.

I remember looking at my cards and *knowing* I had the winning hand before any other action happened. Even before the 'flop' (the first three cards turned over in the community pot) the betting was uncharacteristically loose. There was a few hundred dollars in the pot at this $2/$4 table. The flop came and the Queen and Jack of hearts in my hand was matched with the King and Ten of hearts. I had a royal flush draw. There were only two other players left in the hand after the lead bet. Now there was over a thousand dollars in the pot. People started gathering around to watch what was happening. I made the decision to stay in.

I mean, my guides gave me the *knowing* that I had the best hand and so far, so good. "Call."

The next card was the nine of hearts. NINE. A FREAKING NINE OF CUPS! You see, the modern playing card deck is based on the Tarot. Hearts in the common Bicycle deck are Cups in Tarot. The meaning of the card? Contentment, satisfaction, the end of an accomplishment. The number nine in numerology represents the end of a cycle and finality. Signs, signs, everywhere the signs. BOOM! Right there, straight flush. I couldn't lose.

And then it happened.

Free will is something I talk often about. I was completely in control of my actions. I was inundated with the energy of the table. Heart beating heavy. Everything was in slow motion; the chips being shuffled by players. The pit bosses looking me over with head nods to their colleagues.

Check around at the table. I thought I would trap on the 'river' (the last community card). The last card comes out and it doesn't matter. I have the nuts, the best hand possible without a chance to lose. "Tony" goes all in and I don't flinch. He's trying to intimidate everyone at the table with a bully move or get paid. The other player folded instantly. ALL EYES ON ME.

Then I saw Tony's daughter. Their house and his soon to be ex-wife standing in the middle kitchen, as he explained how he thought I was bluffing if I called. The tears, the loss of safety, the anger and the disappointment. I held Tony's future in my next action. I sat there for almost five minutes and everyone was hush. The pot was piled in front of me. I looked into Tony's eyes, his knee shaking, his hands clasped in front of his mouth. He was praying.

Hail Mary, full of grace. "You need to go home and take care of your daughter Kayleigh. Fold."

I pushed my cards face down towards the dealer as all the onlookers erupted. I heard, "Oh my God, how could you do that!" and "Jesus, that was a Hollywood bluff." Suddenly one of the onlookers reached over the dealer, grabbed my cards and turned them over for the players, pit bosses and world to see. Now what he did, showing someone else's fold cards, is one of the biggest no-no's in poker. Second only to folding the nuts. It alludes to rigging the game to move chips to another person at the table, that you may be working with, while hustling everyone else. Although I 'knew' Tony, I had only met him at the table a few hours earlier.

At this point, the eruption turned into an explosion. Chips were flying, security was pushing through, the pit bosses were grabbing my arms. Ugh. I thought I had done the right thing. Thanks for the lesson, Universe. I spent the next three hours in a two-way mirror room with a Lawrence Fishburne looking dude, that wanted me to confess that it was a scam we just ran. He was shouting at me, asking how I knew Tony's daughter's name and why would I fold that much money with that hand. Meanwhile, Tony was in another room getting berated after winning the best hand of his life. Even the police were in and out as an intimidation tactic. I confessed. "I'm a Medium. I use my ability at the table. There is no collusion and I'm not trying to deceive anyone." By now they had watched the tape of all I had done that day. The clean-up at the blackjack table, the tournament that didn't happen and several hours at the cash table. They walked me to the door and told me never to return. Not even to visit the buffet. When they let me go, Tony was sitting on the hood of his car near the exit, smoking a cigarette. I walked up to him but kept my distance.

"What the hell was that all about!! What were you thinking!!" He was half angry, half sarcastic as poker players live in the gloat.

I looked at him and realized he wasn't getting any of this, at all. I cleared my throat. "When your mother died of lung cancer four years ago, she told you that she wanted you to be a 'Simple Man'. You need to take care of your family and most importantly your daughter, Kayleigh. She said that you would lose the house if you didn't come home big today."

Tony looked at me and started to cry. He said how sideways things had been since his mom passed. How he didn't feel worthy to even be a dad and how terrible he is at it. His long drags on his cigarette tempered his breathing.

"Josephine, right?" I asked.

"No, that's her middle name."

"I'll take it," I said.

Before I walked to my car to never walk into that casino again, Tony made the announcement that he was quitting gambling and going home to figure it out. I don't know what happened to him after that, but I know he was headed in the right direction. I was beginning to recognize that spirit put me in places, to meet people and part of their path to show them something, even if it meant taking the brunt of the punishment.

Mechanical Resonance

Things are put into our path for a reason. For me, it was music, comedy and the arts. I certainly enjoyed music and just like a spiritual gift, you look at your parents as an influence. My dad was the cool guy on a naval ship. In the Navy, when you were out at sea for months on end in the late 60's, you found the guy with a reel to reel so you could hear music in the isolation tin. During childhood, you found the friend with a pool. In college, you found the person on your floor with a car.

When I found the box of oversized reels, it was like finding a treasure trove of nostalgia and influence. I fired up the reel to reel, learned how to load it up, figured out the maintenance and gave it a go. I pressed play and felt the excitement of all that lived within music. It sounded like a muffled tin can, but as the opening riff of "Whole Lotta Love" came out the sides of that beast box, I fell in love with what I heard. By the time "Moby Dick" was halfway through, I knew what I wanted to do with music. John Bonham became a constant in my life and everything Zeppelin touched was my interest.

Music and comedy became the backdrop of what could keep my attention. It made me discover the world of expression and the larger world beyond in the emotion it created. If it wasn't for Anthrax, I may never have read a Stephen King novel. Metallica opened the door for me to discover Hemmingway and understand Passover. Iron Maiden helped me find Crimea on the map and I would never have known what the "Light

Brigade" was. Nor would I have the appreciation for the plight of Native Americans, Alexander the Great or the Gordian Knot. It wasn't all heavy. James Taylor made me read up on prisoner deportation in Australia. Gordon Lightfoot and Crosby, Stills and Nash shed light on civil unrest. Don McLean and Billy Joel gave a full history lesson in less than five minutes.

I was the kid that read the liner notes. I would listen to the music and liked it based on the feel and their words. The literal as well as the vibration. I was interested in the art and science of creating.

So, when the sing a long hair metal band Tesla came on the scene, I was more than ready to receive a message for my path. They were a straightforward, dual guitar driven, good ole rock and roll band. Born at a time when power ballads became survival to do what they loved as a career. My first foray into their world was "Modern Day Cowboy" a song about the cold war and playing chicken with nuclear power. But as a kid hooked on drumming, it was the energy of the song, the catchiness and oh yeah, the 26' Paiste Gong behind drummer, Troy Lucketta. For most bands, the gong was a showpiece a la Bonham. But not in Tesla's debut single. The song ended with the ring out of a solid center strike that outlasted the guitar reverb and vocals.

I fell in love with the band to get to the man.

In their follow up album, they practically said, the music isn't the message here, it's the inventor. "Edison's Medicine" is about Nikola Tesla's life. Blazing with a musical instrument I had never heard of, let alone thought would be on a rock album.

The Theremin was a featured instrument. The Theremin was invented with Tesla mathematics and was the only musical instrument he played. It used energy fields to create sound relative to where you placed your hands. My interests were peaked across the board. I needed to know.

When I read "Man Out of Time" by Margaret Cheney, everything began to make sense in a new way. I discovered his inventions, The Great Radio Controversy and of course the Current Wars with businessman, Thomas Edison. Growing up in the shadows of GE headquarters in upstate New York, Edison was worshiped as a pioneer, innovator, and humanitarian. After a deep dive into how he conducted his business, specifically with Westinghouse and Tesla, he was a thief, an opportunity capitalist and a rather cruel human being. Tesla had a naivete about him that caught him up in the wonder of what he was capable of inventing and discovering. He was the conduit of energy. And everyone either used him, made fun of him or didn't respect him. Thomas Edison was the worst, but the list was long and distinguished. I was angry at first, but I remember sitting there thinking about both sides. There was good reason why Edison had such polarity, he might have had good intention but was lured by the intent of business deals and ownership. He hardly created anything, he simply was the underwriter. He was the first and best example of Energy Laundering. He took other people's ideas and turned them into his own. Without Tesla, Edison wouldn't have had the inventions. Without Edison, the world would not have known many of Tesla's inventions. The sin was, Edison claimed it was his when it went to market, never giving Tesla credit until the proof was shown.

I could easily write an entire book on Nikola Tesla because of my study of him, my adoration and most importantly, my understanding of his behavior. I wanted to know HOW he was inspired to make his inventions. It took reading many books until I discovered his actual techniques. On the surface, he was an insomniac, a madman that allowed himself to be driven by an OCD like behavior for numbers and a routine that bordered on superstition. What he was really doing, was channeling and worshiping the very energy structure that all machines were built on. Steam engines, electricity, even humans.

His mind weaved through the understanding of ratios and the building structure of 3, 6, 9. He could see it, like numbers on a page. It is why he has over 1,000 inventions to his name and was stolen from regularly. He didn't care about the money, he cared about the human application of the machinery. He was so far ahead of his time that many of his theoretical inventions didn't come into fruition until technology caught up. Some say it didn't happen until the Roswell crash, but that's another book.

Tesla's technique however, was something to marvel at and where I learned so much. He would nap for a short time and then began to journal either new inventions or solutions to problems where other ideas had stalled. Those naps were his only rest, never sleeping more than four hours a day and never more than 90 minutes at a time. He journaled so much that when he died, the US Government seized over 40,000 volumes of his work. What would the government need with the writings of a near penniless, relatively homeless man with no family and no assets? His life was a casualty of brilliance.

When I finish my book on Tesla the Medium, it will be rich with examples of events and people in his life that gave hard lessons to a gentle Aquarian soul that wanted the best for humanity, but had his soul sucked dry by the structure and time he was born into. For this book, I can explain that his ability to channel, meditate and then create, is the lesson I needed to learn. I can't hold a candle to his mathematical brilliance. On top of the dozens of books and other resources I've read, I've learned about his life in depth. His chart speaks about a man here for the common good. Gifted with a work ethic and drive to achieve, but cursed with an inability to understand the human condition which left him prone to be taken advantage of and lead a lonely existence. But it all had purpose. When I saw his chart for the first time, I noticed Tesla had a polarity to him as well. It made him who he was. This mad genius that couldn't associate with some, but was so driven to bring things to light, he couldn't help himself to be distant and taken advantage of his whole life.

Nikola Tesla taught me that brilliance doesn't make you adored and people will take advantage of you no matter what. That's human nature's pit fall, survival. He showed me that just because you see things so radically different, doesn't mean you are a freak. But it will make you a target. People will surround you that don't understand you and will want to take advantage of you. That's the human side. The Aquarian side showed me that we all have a mission for the greater good. Your gift must be used for good. There is a bigger plan at play here.

Nate the Great

There is a belief that the soul is on a cosmic arc which brings you to different incarnations of self for the experiences that your soul needs to fulfill its purpose. In each of those reincarnations, we make a soul contract in which we are given strengths and challenges. They project in our house and planetary placements, life path numbers and birthday. Each soul contract includes our soul family, both living and in spirit. Our birthdate and time have an exact placement in the universe that will never, ever happen again. Recognize how unique we all are. More unique than a fingerprint and DNA.

It is a belief that we choose our path. My choice for a dad came in the form of Nate. As I mentioned before, coming from a land locked state and heading to the high seas was something you needed to be built for. His sense of humor evolved from the slightly inappropriate to full on dad joke heaven. Adventure, humor and optimism. A true Sagittarius.

"I don't know, but yeah, I'd like to go," is how we ended the discussion about his mother passing at the age of 85. Losing a parent, no matter your age, is still a shock to the system. I was trying to figure out whether to get him a plane ticket to St. Paul or to drive out there with him.

My phone rang a moment later and it was my Aunt Caroline. "So, yeah, are ya goin', or no?" Her Minnesota accent sounded like a Canadian hockey fan on the way to the Mankato, in an accent that emphasizes the vowel and never seems to stick the landin'. "Yeah, so, if you're comin', you're the minister and everything."

My dad and I were headed to the land of 10,000 lakes and had two days to get there. I also had a punchy drive to write a eulogy for a woman I had only met six times in my life. Most of those were before I was nine. She was a gruff and tumble woman. Having a mouth like a sailor was likely the best training my father could have had. She smoked, drank, and played bingo. Oh, and she had kids. Nine of them.

Grandma Grace was great at setting you up for the fall with a cutting sense of humor. It was her way of showing you that she cared. It was only fitting that my grandfather was nothing short of a Capricorn saint. Grounding everyone. We didn't mistake his kindness or docile approach for weakness. He stood his ground. Even after Grace left him, she later returned with two kids that he agreed to raise. You wouldn't have known that the two youngest weren't his. The family assimilated, as it was an understanding early on that family was family. There were no blurred lines. I found strength in that as an adoptive father.

Road trips with my dad were always the best. The radio was our friend. We loved to hear the different radio announcers for local baseball games, no matter the team, affiliation or level.

We'd find a station that had the right mix of rock and 'oldies,' and if we found the local NPR station, we'd get Car Talk or Old Time Radio replays from the 1940's and 50's.

Static Buzz "The Philco Delco R-1227 is the last radio your family will ever need, with its sleek design and superior phonic reception."

"You know my father used to work on those all the time." My dad looked out the window at the flat farm landscape somewhere between Buffalo and Chicago. "We had parts everywhere, drove my mom crazy."

*** Philco Radio Time presents... the Bing Crosby Show (Applause) ***

"This used to be on Friday nights. It was Ma's bowling night, so he would come home to be around the kids and we'd sit in front of the radio with him. Kathy would be on his lap and Ricky, Me and Stu would be skewn around the floor. I think Kenny was a baby or it was even before then." My dad's accent came back the more he spoke. Some people have a soft spot for their mothers. My dads was definitely for my grandfather. Even when I asked him about my grandmother on the drive, his replies would be about my grandfather and his relationship to her. It wasn't anything bad, it just solidified how much my grandma Grace was a difficult person. Knowing her was like hugging a porcupine. You had to go about it the right way, or you'd get stuck with a quill.

We talked about everything and got onto the topic of past lives. My dad had a Navy buddy, Ron. Ron ended up a trucker when he got back to the states and they shared the most elaborate schemes. They did things that only two crazy military guys could do before responsibility and coming of age set in. They decided to hitchhike from port to Oklahoma so Ron could get married. It was a complicated story about going a few miles from here to there and somehow getting from Florida to Texarkana. They lucked out and got a ride in the back of a limo, drinking aged scotch with an Oil Baron who got them as far as Stillwater. My dad told me all about making sure he got Ron to the aisle just in time, but that he hardly remembered it.

He also talked about knowing the town like the back of his hand, without ever having stepped foot in Oklahoma. "It was the funniest thing, I knew where the hall was, the pharmacy and even the post office." He wowed them with the details he knew, the turns you needed to take to wherever they mentioned. He was describing either a past life or a pre-cognizance of simply knowing. He had a knack for it, but it was never encouraged or explored. I gave him the open door to talk about it. Part relief, part realization that I was his son for a reason. As much as I loved the road trips to ballparks and concerts, this one had a heaviness that he had run away from years ago. This one was cathartic. We talked more than we listened. We tried to remember as much as we could of "Who's on First" and as much as we tried to stay in our lane, we would end up saying each other's line and laughing.

"I don't know... THIRD BASE," said in unison was always a great punchline. Funny and healing.

Right on schedule, we ended up on the other side of Chicago and well into Wisconsin. The conversation and Cubs game moved us along to the Brewers game, who were playing on the west coast. So, driving 18 hours to the Dells made us crash at 2 AM. When we woke up my dad's tone was, "Yeah, we gotta get there but we totally don't have to rush." Which meant, we really should get there. We grabbed breakfast at an Alpine Breakfast Haus and ate like kings. Pancakes, sausage, bacon, gravy, toast, eggs, omelets, coffee, juice, pastries and fruit. We literally gorged ourselves. When the bill came, I remembered I pulled enough money together for a budget to get there and back on. I cringed at the sight of the bill, but as I turned it over, I was shocked at the total. $11.92. Was there another bill? Did they forget to add on everything we ordered from the left side of the menu? I have never had so much value in one meal. It was divine satisfaction. Not just the price, but watching my dad eat sausage gravy on biscuits like it was his job.

We walked out of the A-Framed restaurant and looked across the street. A grand Indian Reservation Casino. Now, this was years before I learned how my gift was meant to be used, so, I viewed it as a stop to honor my recently deceased gamblin' grandma. My dad smiled and shook his head. We walked into the smoke-filled playground where all the bells and whistles were going off. I walked up to the Blackjack table and threw down about half of what I had.

My dad nervously laughed and said, "How are we going to get home?" "Watch this," I said as I rolled out my bet that was fueled by syrup and bacon.

After a half hour of strategically betting erratically with fluctuations of the minimum to the maximum. From double down to let it ride. I built a stack five times as high as where I started. It drew a decent crowd considering it was before noon in a casino. It also attracted the Pit Boss. I wasn't doing anything 'wrong' but I was clearly there for the score. My dad leaned in and said, "I think we're going to be late."

I smiled and said, "They can't start without me." Having the Eulogy shift, had its benefits.

As we cashed in, we had the casino escort follow at a distance. This is the one that keeps an eye on you while you're winning, to either direct you to the next highest table game to see if you're working with anyone else, or wish you a good day as you put them in the red for the morning.

"We got our White Castles," I said shaking the money at him. We both laughed and took to the road again. Over the next few days, we assimilated with the family we knew. For my dad it was like old times, seeing his brothers and sisters. For me, it was talking to my 45 FIRST cousins. Yeah, I didn't know all their names either. It's more like a feeling of comfort and home, being accepted by strangers you know and have connections with. Even if you didn't have all that much in common. We went out every night, ate Juicy Lucy burgers and did cousin karaoke. Here's what I learned.

When it came to my grandma Grace, she was a hard woman. Her words cut deeply and were to the point. Words from another era; mildly racist, derogatory, and mean. In contrast, she was ferocious when defending the family. Both could be unforgivable or rationalized. In the end, you always knew where you stood with her. Good, bad or indifferent.

At the funeral, there were over 30 cars and numerous people. She was buried between her first and third husbands. Being a military funeral, there was little time for the Minnesota goodbyes. Those are the ones that take 2-3 hours because, "I forgot to tell ya" or "You know what, I've been meanin' to ask ya somethin'." It was quick and dirty, the dichotomy that was just like Grace. Until then, I had focused on her flaws, the way she lived her life, the way she spoke to people and the judgement that came with multiple marriages. What I learned was that family is a beautiful mess. Formed from the stars and destined by the synchronicities. What we do with them is the real challenge.

House of Love

1,946 days. That's how long my oldest son was in foster care. A badge of honor for most foster parents. A statistic to me as this was about a higher calling.

The Spiritual community boasts the most ostentatious ways of helping others. Amazing stories about readings that occurred spontaneously at the grocery store, an unlikely animal rescue, and oh, let's not forget the essential oil that saved someone at the gas station. They help everyone they meet and now they have another satisfied customer in their upline and be sure to follow them for more life hacks around the actual work.

Although there is a place for everything, I'm pointing out there is a vast difference between those that talk about 'doing the work' and ACTUALLY doing the work. It is often mistaken that your personal agenda is the only process in which you obtain enlightenment or soul purpose. There are bold statements that we discover about our self-worth and the value our gifts bring to the world. The mistake we make is a lack of humbleness for the process. The mistake is thinking that each epiphany is the top of the mountain, where the truth is, when really, the summit is many more years up the path. Celebrate where you are and realize it is a milestone and not a finish line.

You must understand that last line to understand the journey of being a foster parent. You must absorb the entire paragraph above to understand the difference between saying you do light work and being a light worker. It's a fallacy to think that becoming an adoptive parent is like the play "Annie" or to be a foster parent is like being Sandra Bullock in the movie "The Blind Side" or a weekly episode of TVs "This is Us." Although heartfelt adaptations, the real work is much deeper than an eight-minute montage about running away, or a breakthrough occurring in 42 minutes to give you enough resolve to want to learn more. It is every day. It is dealing with a constant threat of safety while creating identity. It is explaining that there are more people in the world that love you. It is the ongoing struggle and triumph of getting and staying ahead of becoming defined by your circumstances.

Becoming an adoptive or foster parent is an opportunity to fulfill one's life path and break karmic cycles.

The reasons to become a foster parent have many facets. Some decide to follow that path because they simply want to help and contribute to making a difference. Others find it to be an act of charity to model for others how to put kindness into action. For me, it was a process of understanding loss and purpose.

Tracey's strength as a partner was the ability to flow with the idea that anything is possible. After years of 'trying', it was clear that adoption was the best and viable route to having children as part of our lives.

There are several options out there for adoption. A lot of the adoption services are ready to help and are good at several things. First, finding children whose parent(s) want to give them up. This is usually by unwed mothers that consulted on having a choice. Giving up a child is the right thing to do according to their propaganda because it is what God wants. Plus, there are many financial considerations, such as they pay for healthcare and extras. Second, and more powerfully, making sure the adoptive family is Christian. Requirements for this include, a 'traditional marriage' (man and woman), and frequent and active participation in a Christian Church. Their matching process was sincerely about the right fit.

Let's not mince words, we were white, straight and had a double income. I was amazed at how organized and clear they were in their efforts. By comparison, going through the channels of foster care and a county agency, who are underfunded, under resourced and unable to focus on the 'best fit' but rather the safe fit, scared many away.

The process is overloaded and included home inspections, classes on parenting and home visits from start to post completion. Even the strongest of couples and families feel the strain of judgement. Not to mention the paperwork that you sign, giving the agency full authority to surprise you with a visit, or question your lifestyle and the 'fit' of a placement at any time. They can also remove the placement(s) at any time, for a reason as small as a field office decision. The classes that certify you talk a lot about your style, setting rules and boundaries and of course, loss. Because the goal of foster parenting is reunification with the biological family, not to give you a family. So, to be under the microscope for virtually everything in your life, without the guarantee of being emotionally destroyed, is strain beyond words.

The fear for me was real. I'm a freakin' Medium. All it would take was one bible beating, teetotaler to make a fuss and it was over. To hear the horror stories about County Case workers making poor decisions was rampant, and was rivaled only by a court system that sometimes focused on the anomaly rather than the right thing. To say there were sleepless nights is an understatement.

Early in the placement, I had to go to the county building to drop off paperwork and I was nervous about someone saying something, being recognized or worse, being called out for what I did. There are times when Spirit has things happen in a way that lets you know you are in the right place. It comes in the form of Déjà vu, like signs, numbers or music. In this case it was who I saw. As I walked into the large bullpen style office, I saw in the reception area someone I had just seen at a recent show. I had actually read her.

Minutes later, another person walked by and said hello because she recognized me. She had been at a home party a few months earlier. The records person came out to take my paperwork and recognized me from a YouTube video. Then another person came out to say how impactful a reading I had given her friend was, and how it had helped her, and she couldn't wait to book an appointment. In other words, I had nothing to worry about. The third floor of the Office of Protective and Family Services of Albany County knew me and who I was. They were celebrating that I was involved in the foster care system. Although I was working through an agency, County oversight is a paramount part of the process. This gave me solace that I was in the right place and everything would work out.

After School Special...

We started as eligible for respite service. Respite is a term used in foster care that means the placement family needs support for a placement. It could be to sort out a situation or even to go on vacation. When we met Martin, he came to us for a weekend from his current situation. We sat him down and went over the rules. In our house there were two rules; be safe and don't be hungry. The refrigerator was full, video games were in his room and curfews were agreed upon.

Martin is culturally different from us. He had been placed into foster care after his mother abandoned him and his older brother a few years before. He was twelve when his mother packed the house up after he went to school one morning and left for Texas. He came home late because of an after-school program that he didn't want to be in. Martin and his 16-year-old brother found nothing left but their beds. His brother was resourceful. He cut corners and hustled to pay rent and to provide for him and Martin, until the landlord started to ask questions. The power company shut off the electricity and eventually, his brother was caught cutting too many corners and was headed to jail. Martin lost his entire family in a matter of months.

So, these two shiny foster parents decided to do something fun with a kid who had grown up on the other side of the tracks. What did we do? Brought him to a rodeo. Yep, a good ole fashion, calf catching rodeo. I remember how awkward he looked, pulling up his pants to walk up the bleachers to sit. He did it though and even lied to us to tell us how great it was. He was gracious and kind, but you could tell this experience was another example of how he didn't fit into this world. However, we stayed in contact. A few months after his respite time with us, he called my cell phone from a payphone. "Hey, Br-Brandon. It's Martin. I'm at Stewarts and I don't got nowhere to go." I picked him up in a driving, freezing rain on an early December night. It felt like an "After School Special" episode. He was beyond a good kid, but wasn't perfect. I'm a good foster parent, but beyond perfect. It was a match in heaven.

After proving that awkwardness was our greatest offense, our lives really changed.

We had been in conversations to be considered to be a newborn placement. The family of four kids were already in care and a newborn was on the way. The challenge was a biological mother with sincere mental health issues and a father that simply didn't have the tools to overcome them and take care of children. I had been attending meetings for placement and ongoing care.

The goal was to have the newborn as well as one of the older children placed with us, in order to keep two of the brothers together. The relationship with the other foster parents connected to the case was important, as we planned to get the kids together on a regular basis.

Leaving the Train Station

"Congratulations, it's a boy!" The caseworker let us know he was a healthy baby boy, the paperwork was already filed and come tomorrow, we'd be responsible for a living thing. Before you think I'm being facetious, know that it had accelerated from nothing to everything, and staying humble was very important. After sitting in on regular meetings for months, I knew much about what we were facing. We had given them confidence that we could do everything new parents would be capable of. Caring, decision making and providing them with a life that would be amazing and full of adventure.

Being a foster parent means that you always need to be ready. Ready for any change coming, going, loss, emotions, everything. You found yourself using skills you didn't know you had. You also had to learn skills you had no idea you needed. With the foster care system consisting of primarily elementary to high school aged children, the thought of getting a toddler was a stretch, and a newborn seemed almost impossible. None of the training was centered around a newborn. It was centered around understanding traumas and managing behaviors of kids that were conditioned to never feel safe because they didn't know where their next bed would be. On the first night, Tracey and I spent the entire time trying to coddle a newborn because we hadn't learned how to swaddle in any of those classes. The first night takes years off your life.

I had dreamed of him before I met him. When I talked about having children, the 'Z' stuck on my tongue. Zachary, Zoe, Zion. I could never quite make it out when Spirit told me. So, when his name Alexander was on the paperwork, I was like, "What the hell, Spirit?" The nurse then suggested calling him Alex or maybe Zander. It stopped me in my tracks, and I smiled. Spirit had me on this one.

I remember holding him and understanding what the world was about. He was helpless, defenseless and taken from a woman who loved him deeply but couldn't provide for him. He didn't have any ailments or side effects from her inability to mentally care for herself. He was healthy, strong, and simply needed someone to take him, hold him and show him the world. I always had the night shift and holding him to get him through the night was an amazing experience. I felt my own connection grow with him, and with Spirit.

Shortly after Zander arrived, Chayanne came to us. Though his transition was planned, it was still a curve ball being thrown at us. Chayanne had a lot of adjusting. This was the seventh house he had lived in, and he had just turned five. He was also going from being the second oldest child, to becoming the oldest. The complicated but necessary plan for the immediate sibling group, removed him from his two other brothers and sister, who went to another family. The reasons were many, but in short, it was a five-child sibling group with each having specific needs and subsequent traumas. It would be too much for any one family unit to manage. The other foster parents, Rose and Tim, and Tracy became family over it. We all accepted the mission to have the kids know one another.

I had had dreams of being near a train station off and on my whole life. It would look like a scene from a movie where I saw the steam rise around a station with a single light. I felt like I was creeping around, trying not to be seen or caught. But it was more of a feeling than rational reason. After Zander came, I kept having the dream and it was more intense. It was about feelings and language. German, definitely German. Angry, disposable feelings. A constant worry of being caught. I felt like I was protecting this child. It was my mission to protect him and get him to safety. I knew my role as a father figure. I knew I was in search of understanding whether these dreams were messages of metaphor or of a past life.

Chayanne, like many five-year-old's, was obsessed with trains. When it came to having a child with behavioral challenges, your support is everything. Mrs. Bennet was the right combination of structure and encouragement that complimented what we had at home. We never would have made it, if it wasn't for the incredible support from all the teachers at his Elementary School. You supported us in a way that can never be repaid.

Chayanne loved Thomas the Train. All trains really. But in Mrs. Bennet's room, was this amazing train table that was the perfect encouragement for a kid who was impulsive and needed to be rewarded for getting it together. We did it all. Train shows, lists of all the trains we had, which ones were missing and we watched "The Polar Express" more times than "The Big Lebowski." That's the best way to describe the shift in becoming a parent. I went from quoting The Dude to singing about Hot Choc-o-late!

As Zander got older, he wanted to be just like his brother. He fell in love with the trains just as easily. In the world of hand-me downs, he had every one of them at his disposal. He watched Thomas give lessons on friendship and hard work. So, when I saw a trauma response to trains, I needed to take note.

Living in an upstate New York mill-town, the train runs right along the Hudson River from New York City to Montreal. For years, we heard the train come through town. It's the type of sound that ends up in the background and you grew to hardly notice it. I would point it out from time to time, but Zander always kept his eyes on the screen. One day, the train whistled through about mile from our house. Only I didn't hear it, but Zander did.

"Whoot, Whoot," went the standard call and response for a train approaching a populated area.

Zander jumped up and went behind the coffee table and couch. It was one of his favorite places for stuffed animals and hide and seek. He tucked himself under the blanket, gripping it behind his head. "I'll find you," I said thinking he was being impromptu and wanting attention. I pulled blanket back to his shriek and tears. "NOOOOOOO!!"

"Whooooooooooooooot, Whooooooooooot, Whoot, Whoot," the train was almost to town.

"I don't want to go!!!" He screamed in some verbal dialect and looked up at me as if he going off to slaughter. His head and whole body were shaking. The tears flowed and his mouth laid open as he quietly cried. He couldn't talk. He couldn't breathe.

I picked him up against his protest and held this beautiful 3-year-old boy, who was gripped with an irrational fear. I held him as he sobbed uncontrollably, shaking and trying to hide. I could only hold him to keep him safe.

He looked up at me with a beat red face, "The train, here?" he asked in a rough whisper.

"No, no, you're here with me now." He nestled into me again and his crying became a soft whimper.

"Whooooooooooooooot, Whooooooooooot, Whoot, Whoot," as it whipped through the center of town.

"Ahhhhhhhhh!!" he screamed into my chest. I held him tightly and said it was going to be ok. I closed my eyes and I was brought into a film noir scene as I held him tight. I just wanted it to go away for him, whatever this fear was. I looked up and saw the soldier standing there. His outline mostly, in false regality, poised and in control. My gloved hand extended the envelope and he peered into it. I couldn't understand what he was saying in his condescending tone. "That's all of it," I said. He nodded at what was behind me. Under my coat, the child.

"This one is mine."

He cursed me in German and spit on the ground. I was waiting for a bullet to the chest. I looked down with my eyes closed. I felt myself move quickly between the train cars. The rush of adrenaline. The fear of loss and the whirlwind of processing what was being shown to me.

I held him tightly.

"Whoot, Whoot," the train was on to the next town and the doppler effect let me know it was moving away.

I felt Zander by my side as he slipped over my leg and onto the couch, the blanket covering him. He was trying to curl his way behind me.

"You're ok, you're OK!" I said holding his face. He gave me a nod, "I know." He looked around and saw the living room he called home. He pushed away from me and picked up a train and waved his finger at it. "That's not nice," and walked to the kitchen and put it in the garbage. I never took it out.

Never Surrender

In the complicated world of foster care, there are standards and rules. It takes into account parental rights as well as the rights of the children. The parents have the right to overcome the challenges that the county welfare deems needing improvement. And the children have the right to safety, security and permanency. In New York State, the rule for permanency is 15 out of 22 months. In other words, within two years, the parent needs to provide placement for their children for 15 months in order to drop an investigation. It also means. that if the child is placed for that amount of time in foster care without progress of the parent, then they are moved from the status of 'reunification' to the goal of 'permanency'. Ultimately, in that moment the rights of the children out-weigh the rights of the parents. We were in the final phases of parental termination and there was only one thing that could push it back, another child.

I want to be clear on one thing. Foster parents have zero rights. We are literally spectators of what can become of our hearts. Decisions made by judges, legal guardians and case workers can be gut wrenching and biased. After years of changing lawyers, renewing motions and 'extraneous' circumstances needing review, the goal of the court is to reunify the children with their biological family. The goal of a foster parent is to become everything the children need without question or interference.

By the time a new judge was appointed, and the case finally started moving forward, we had another brother in the mix, Eric. We were already dealing with one child that had moved seven times, and had finally created stability, as well as a newborn. Did we really want another? It would upset the apple cart. It would add two more years onto the 18 we signed up for. Neither one of us had slept for over two years. The answer was a hundred times, yes. When he arrived, his mother was well aware of what was going to happen. She also knew that if something happened to the newborn, the case would be over in a heartbeat. Again, the fear of what could happen was front and center. The biological mother did what anyone who needed to do the right thing to try and keep her child, would do. She knew that if she went through 'normal' channels, she would lose another child. She was creative while reinforcing her lack of stability. The foster families and the case workers were concerned for the coming baby and what the biological mother might do.

The thought of all this was heart wrenching. Both sides, the biological mother and the foster parents were buried in fear.

She decided to try and have Eric in the back of a medical center's library. A Code White was called when she tried to have a baby in the 'Non-Fiction Resources' section. In my corny sense of humor, I wanted to rename him Dewey. Get it? Library, Dewey decimal? It's not funny if I have to explain it. However, the name Eric was a nice mix of what his parents wanted and a common friend Tracey and I had growing up.

Eric is bright and shiny and the equilibrium of energy between the kid that bounces of the walls and the other that cries all the time. When he entered the 'court proceedings' he would have almost no interactions with his biological parents because of the number of times, they tried to pull one over on case workers and the courts.

There were 74 court hearings and proceedings before all the children were released for adoption. Some of the hearings were procedural or for updates, but rarely were there any decisions. Some of the hearings were about all six in the sibling group, some were about only the youngest two, Eric and Zander. As the walls closed in, the discussion of surrender was on the table. The biological parents had run out of legal moves. They were no longer able to fire their court appointed representation. They were no longer able to file motions on the legitimacy of the court as they did early in the case. The biological father cited a very long and complex case that involved Native American tribes, and the lineage placement of the child with the family or tribe, as opposed to county systems. It pushed the case back years and was eventually dismissed without grounds.

The lawyers were disgusted with the move. I saw it as another way he loved his kids. He was doing everything he could to stay in their lives longer.

On the day of the final court appearance, the biological mother surrendered her rights. This allowed her to negotiate having contact with her children and staying in their lives. A few visits a year, school pictures and updates. It was the right thing to do. This woman was the portal for the children I am raising. I never understood the bombastic and punitive way people talked about hurting a biological parent when they fell down. The judgement and cruelty. The responsibility was shifting and we were soon to be the stewards of what was best for the children. Knowing their story was important. Connecting with so many people that are hurt or broken because they don't know their story, was gut wrenching. I didn't want to do that to these boys.

We came into the court room the usual way. I sat in the gallery. The biological father sat by himself. The judge called the court to order and announced the proceeding. She announced that this was a judgement rule on behalf of the children. She declared her intent on terminating the rights of the biological parent. She explained in detail what that would mean.

"This means, you will not have any more supervised visits. This means you will not see your children grow up. It means that as of today, you will not have the responsibility of these children. I would encourage you to discuss with your counsel the very reasonable offer put forth by the court, agreed to by the Russ' and without abandon, the right thing to do. I ask you again to surrender your rights."

"I will NEVER SURRENDER!" he said pounding the table with one fist. He spoke through gritted teeth. He sat there with dream catcher earrings on and an ascot covering his throat. The medium in me saw everything. I understood where he was.

I got the attention of the law guardian and pulled her over. The law guardian asked for a chamber with the foster parents included. When I had all of the lawyers together, I explained what was going on.

"Is there another word the judge can use aside from surrender?"

"Why the hell are we talking about this?" his attorney asked.

"He's living out a past life. I've seen it before with his kids. Changing the word, will change the dynamics." After an hour delay and a few law students going through the Lexus Nexus database, the judge ruled that as a matter of practicum, the word surrender could not be substituted for any reason. The biological father had only two outcomes, surrender or termination. He chose termination.

As the judge read the decision, there were ten swords being driven into his heart. The ten of swords is a tremendous burden, self-inflicted wounds and the pain of choices, ancestral trauma and defeat. I felt every sword. He yelled back at her in a language he had no control over, the lawyers shouted and with one hit of the gavel, the whole room went silent.

I make jokes about adopting kids who were left unattended or that we picked them up from the kennel. Truth is, these are my kids for a reason. I could write an entire book just about all the wonderous moments I've had with each of them. I have a very distinct and specific role to each of them and them to me. I also understand that I had a role in breaking the cycle so the healing could start.

Shortly after the termination, came the adoption. Not long after that, I brought the boys to see their biological father, because it was the right thing to do.

Rest Stop Reiki

I have been on a quest to understand my gifts and how to apply them. In a quiet moment, I have struggled to understand my own energy and how to manage it. I had received Reiki a few times but knew little about it as a practice. When I met my Reiki Master Teacher, Jessica, she broke down the history and guided me to understand how to manage my own energy. I am forever in gratitude to her as she helped unlock a part of my physical presence. The meditations, the discipline, and the routine of practice, guided me to understand my own path and the importance of self-care.

After a series of teaching sessions, I elevated to Master Teacher. I had been in a 'healthy choice' mode, finishing off losing my final pounds of over 155 lost. I also had been drinking water like it was my job. Needing to drive over an hour and a half home, I hit the first rest stop on the NYS Thruway. I ushered in and made a direct line to the facilities. As I walked in, there was a woman with a simple haircut, robe and mala beads in her hands. She looked at me, smiled warmly and bowed deep. She broke eye contact, which told me a lot about her intention. She bowed in honor. She stood and nodded hello with everyone else.

As I left the rest room, she was turned to greet everyone as they left. She stopped me with a smile and the thought ran through my mind that I gave at the office and I didn't want to hear about an offer to support an orphanage.

She said in an authentic and ethnic tone, "The Venerable would like to speak to you."

I squinted and nodded. My intuition said, ego off, experience uploading.

I walked up to a man with a red and gold robe. His head was shaved and he was with someone that looked like a clone to my bathroom greeter. She bowed and introduced me.

"Venerable Geshne Lobeshang, this is... "

"I'm Brandon..." I bowed with my eyes to the floor. I looked up at him and he put his hand on my shoulder. He spoke in Tibetan Bohdi language and his interpreter spoke the words.

"You have beautiful energy and you light the world." She paused to hear him speak again.

"You are meant to change the world with your work." She said each word with a smile.

"Your center will become the lessons that you and others need in the world." She nodded her head to me in a deep bow at end of her words.

As it turns out, he was in the inner team of the Dalai Lama and part of the Compassion Tour traveling around the world. To put this into perspective, when I received the Reiki Master Teacher attunement, a Tibetan Monk stopped me to give me encouragement. This has been a magical path so far and this was one of the amazing things that has happened to me.

Happy Phantom

One of the most profound readings I have ever had, was at a 'home party'. A home party is a great way to meet people all at once. At that time, I would meet with individuals one on one. The host would have a gathering and you went to a room separate from them and connect in readings for about a half hour.

It was a murky spring day as I found the house where I would spend the next five hours. It was a middle-class neighborhood with sidewalks, telephone poles and 'drive like your kid lives here' signs.

I could smell the food waft from the front door as it opened. It smelled delicious, as most home parties came with the add on benefit of food. The host was a retired town official and he was one of those guys that was simply nice to everyone. He was jovial as always and let me pick over the buffet for a bite. He showed me to the home office that was built for what we were about to host. As I walked through the living room, the big screen showed whatever NASCAR race was on that weekend and the discussion was about Junior's position and Tony's behavior. I couldn't help but notice one woman sitting there with a cane and a scarf covering her head.

I freaked out a little bit. She was so frail. So weak. So... terminal. Her aura was gray and dark. Like life itself had been sucked out and deposited into a well of despair. Although it's not uncommon for people to be at a home party and not get a reading. I was hopeful and realized I was just scared to have someone like that come to me. A few hours later, Linda came in and sat down. The host helped her into the room, propped her up in a seat, covered her with a blanket and got her a cup of water.

All afternoon I was delivering, "Your grandfather is here," and "Your opportunity is there," and "Your angels are watching over your children." Show. Stoppers.

I tried to find comfort in routine. I tried to control the moment with direction. We joined hands as I said the same connection prayer I always begin with. I felt her **bones** rest in my hands. I opened my eyes and saw the struggle of a woman in her mid-50's, ravished by disease, who only left the house today for the change in scenery. I opened my mouth and nothing came out.

"It's okay, I know. I shouldn't have put you in this position." Linda said to break the tension. "I'm not looking for a miracle, or for you to sugar coat it. I'm stage 4, my body is losing. My time is short."

I looked at her through my tearful eyes. She had more reality than hope. She had every moment of her time being precious, because any Sunday, could be her last Sunday. And she was sitting with me.

"I know not the hour nor the place," I said with my voice crackling. "I'm an optimist about just about everything, but I'm not sure where to take this."

"I want to know about my future," she said matter of factly.

My blood ran cold. I couldn't speak. I just stared. My perspective about what I was doing delivering messages was in peril. I wasn't worth my salt if I couldn't provide comfort in this moment. The FUTURE? She was lucky to make it to Tuesday with what I could see with my human eyes.

"I don't have any illusion of what you see and I don't want to know what will happen to my body." The long pause between was almost unbearable. She changed my perspective almost instantly. "I want to know who I am supposed to help when I pass. I want to be a happy ghost that helps people."

Game changer.

I want the gravity of what she said to sink in. She was facing death and wanted to know how to make something good with her SOUL. She wanted a game plan and to look forward to something. The rest of our time together was about her nieces, her parents that had passed, her connection with the family outside the room and how her battle was much longer than she thought. I saw the energy change about her situation. I saw that her attitude changed her body, her spirit and her path. Her body was embattled and beaten. Her spirit was strong and resilient, and her attitude changed her circumstances. Her aura was becoming brighter with a spark and glow that spread like wildfire. It grew like the Grinch's heart as he lifted the sled over his head and beamed in every direction.

Still sitting in awkwardness, I handed her a crystal from my pocket. It was a Lemurian crystal, the master healer. As I handed it to her, my attempt to make it feel like it wasn't a parting gift, failed. I told her its qualities and that its purpose was healing. She held on to it and said, "I will put it next to my bed then."

Linda survived the week. She even survived the month, the year and many more after. She provided comfort care to others with cancer and loved her pet parrots. Her Facebook posts occasionally put us all on the lookout for a colorful Toucan that somehow got out. She had a smile that made you melt and reminded you that you ARE ALIVE in your body and your SPIRIT is ALIVE within you.

We stayed in touch, and years later, she called me out of the blue. "Stop by, I have something for you." Oh, a present, I thought. But it was a bigger gift than something that could be packaged. When I arrived, she sat me on her couch. Her Toucan flew overhead in the living room.

"Here," she said extending the Lemurian to me. "It's done its job for me and now you need to give it to someone else." I knew what her latest diagnosis was. "Hospice on Monday. I had a hell of a run." Linda stood up and invited me to the kitchen. "Come with me, I have something to show you."

She opened the fridge where she showed me months of supplies of medications.

"Ha... I've been storing up for awhile now... I want to set the record for being in Hospice the longest."

Every Time a Bell Rings...

At a public "Funny You Should Say That!," I try and save the best for last. I always let spirit guide me through the maze of people and their spirits. The woman in the back of the room was up against a plain white wall. I could see the angel wings around her as plain as day. As the evening went on, I delivered many messages and several times I referenced "It's a Wonderful Life." One gentleman had his father come through who regretted that he didn't appreciate what he had and reminded everyone to be grateful for the people in your life. Another woman's father connected and showed how much her mother believed in him and his banking career. He made it after years of struggle. During the entire evening, every time I looked to the back wall, I heard a bell ring. The grade school teacher was the last reading of the night.

"Five." I held up my hand with all my fingers outstretched. "Does five or the month of May make sense to you?"

She shook her head. "No." Matter of factly and without emotion. The wings grew behind her.

"We will go back to that. This angel energy is strong with you, are you a teacher or a care giver?"

"Teacher, grade school." she said relieved that I was connecting to something specific. The wings grew even larger.

"You have an angel behind you." As I said it, I realized there were two pairs behind her. One set hers, one set a protector, a giver of life.

"You have an angel behind you. Who is Michael to you?"

"I don't have a Michael who has passed."

"Middle name. He just said his middle name is Michael."

Her eyes got wide. She pulled out her phone as I continued to talk. She typed furiously and interrupted me with an A-HA moment.

"He is showing me that his lungs are filling up as if he's drowning. He is saying that your mother is here." "OH MY GOD, YES....MICHAEL!" she exclaimed.

The room sat and waited for her to burst into tears. She sobbed openly and nearly went through the whole box of tissues. What we were witnessing was total release. She regained her composure and said, "His first name was Thomas."

"He is showing me military and his pride with it. He is showing me he died in service. He just showed me Clarence from "It's a Wonderful Life." "Yes! Oh my God, yes.. yes... yes..."

"He died for you..." my voice trailed off. "For your mom?"

She sobbed into the rest of the tissues that were left.

She looked up and said, "That is Thomas Michael. He was a West Point Cadet. He drowned while trying to save someone at the beach."

The audience gasped with the reveal.

"Who is he to you?" I asked because he kept showing his connection to her mother, but it wasn't the same mother as her.

"My mother received his lungs after he died."

"I'm sorry, I do this for a living and I can't believe this is happening right now."

The laughter from the crowd lifted the already high energy. She continued to tell the story.

"She was on the donor list for years. She was running out of time and if it didn't happen soon, I would have lost her."

"Did this happen in May?" I was still trying to place the 'five'.

"NOOOOO," she gasped as it hit her all at once. "She only had five percent lung capacity left!"

I hope this angel got its wings. He deserved them.

When You Gotta Go...

As I developed, I found there were certain things that you can ask Spirit for, or things that they can protect you from. In my case, I don't want to know how or when people are going to pass. I often say, "I know not the hour nor the place." But Spirit will show me events that I can't always explain. Things in the future or a connection with 'mile markers' like the birth of a child, a graduation or even a marriage.

Sometimes, they show you that the time that you have with individuals is limited.

I remember the energetic, curious twenty something, come into the room full of life. She was excited about the connection and "just loves this stuff." Her energy was off the chart and as Spirit showed her family, I saw how intuitive her entire family was as well. The family tree moved from one to the other and I gave her specifics as I kept talking like a run-on sentence. "You have three cousins over there, two over here and one of those two just started college and is a bit of a partier. You and your sister are extremely close and the day care connection runs through the family business." She confirmed all of it. The day care center was a center piece for her family and everyone worked there as a rite of passage.

"You have high intuition and you really connect with everyone you meet. You are in a caregiver role. I think you use your intuition in all that you do."

I paused and everything about her was gone. It was like a bulletin coming in. We interrupt this regularly scheduled message for this important bulletin.

"Your aunt is sick." I held up the letter C with my hand. "Cancer," I whispered.

"Yes, my aunt is really sick. As a matter of fact, I'm going there after this reading," she said. "We all love her and she's a really awesome person."

I sat there and stared at her as she talked about her remission and relapse. I literally heard someone say, "Get out, get out now." To a Medium, that is the call to action that you cannot ignore.

"You have to go." I said abruptly, interrupting her. She wondered if she was out of time already. "No, it's not that. Your aunt. You have to go. You need to see her, which is why you are going to see her, correct?"

I didn't wait for an answer. I was already helping her gather her things and walking her to the door. I told her we would reschedule. She was confused, but I cleared it up and told her that we would schedule a full reading after next week. She didn't realize what I was saying. She re-scheduled and we met about two months later.

"So, how is it going?" I asked, knowing what was coming.

Christine looked at me aghast. "Did you know?" I paused and did the middle-aged guy, rolled lips, head nod, shoulder lift. "Well, thank you. I can't tell you how much it meant to me."

Sometimes in readings, the messages you deliver are specific, evidential statements that provide validation of not only you as a Medium, but the person on their path. This was the evidence that timing, is everything.

"I got there just in time. They (her sister and cousin) met me at the car and told me to hurry up. I walked into the room and my mom and other friend moved out of the way for me to get right up next to her." Her crystal blue eyes welled up as she replayed it in her mind. "I took her hand and she let all the air out of her body."

I was receiving the validation that I had done the right thing by making sure that she got there. I really never want to know when or how a person will pass. Frankly, I see enough of HOW people pass. But in this case, the exception was made because it was critical to her life path, who she was and why she feels connection all the time. I couldn't rob her of that. I couldn't be 'right' and say, yeah, your aunt is checking out as we speak. No. She needed the experience more than I needed to keep to my regularly scheduled program.

Namaste Right Here

As a matter of atonement, I take a few days a year where I completely detach and do work for my soul. It is a day where I shut everything out. I tell just a few important people that I'm going dark, so the police don't get called. It is an important thing to shut the world out just a bit for a short time. It gives you clarity. It gives you focus. It helps you prioritize and sift through what is yours and what is others. It is energetic wellbeing. It influences mental wellness, spiritual balance and most importantly, it provides a valve to release the world and its obligations, if only for a minute.

I would take a day and spend it on the land, in meditation and in service. This day I woke up, got dressed, meditated and drove out to the Grafton Peace Pagoda, in silence. They could always use an extra set of hands and you never knew what you would help with when you got there. Building a totem, clearing brush or painting the temple. All could be cathartic and inspiring.

The Grafton Peace Pagoda is a Japanese Buddhist temple of the Nipponzan Myohoji order, built on sacred Mohican land. It is run by volunteers and the steward of the land is Jun Yasuda, a Buddhist Nun. She first became active in the mission of peace in 1978, when she participated in the Longest Walk from San Francisco to Washington, D.C. The walk was in support of Native Americans who were protesting threats to tribal lands and water rights.

The giant domed temple is adorned by the story of Buddha. His struggles, his connection with Creator and humans, and depicts his death and the eight directions. There are over 90 of these types of temples in the world. I will encourage you to find one. Just know, that on the inside of these temples, is nothing. The symbolism of our existence and our plight to make the world notice us.

I had attended a few events there in the past. The people are beyond kind and the experiences have always brought me peace. It is not uncommon for gatherings to happen because parts of the world need peace; Covid, Ukraine, World Trade Center and Nepal. It is a place of Universal Peace for the world.

Na Mu Myo Ho Ren Ge Kyo means, "I take refuge in the Lotus of the Wonderful Law." Without a full history lesson in Buddhism, know it evolved over centuries to understand the Wonderful Law of nature. That is, everything has purpose when it is at peace. The lotus represents the opening and becoming of a beautiful creature on this journey. To chant Na Mu Myo Ho Ren Ge Kyo is an act of faith in the Wonderful Law and in the magnitude of life's inherent possibilities. It is facing your problems head on and instead of blaming others, shifting responsibility or deflecting your own lesson, it embraces the human element of the journey. It allows you to review without the burden of good or bad, without judgement.

When Jun leads the chant, it is for the end of nuclear destruction. She does not judge that her hometown was bombed, her family wiped out and her country turned into a wasteland.

She doesn't look for reparations and doesn't want people to be held accountable.

Jun prays for peace so that it never happens again.

That is how you break a cycle.

So, on the Tuesday morning when I headed up there, I knew it was necessary for me. I needed to sit in the energy of forgiveness, the energy of quiet and the energy of self. When I arrived, I walked up the moderately steep driveway slightly out of breath and found someone gardening at the entrance of the active temple.

"Oh Good! I have to go!" said a middle-aged woman. "I asked for someone to come and finish this up because I need to pick up my son!" She fitted her hat and gave me a few instructions on what to do and what else needed to be done for the day and left.

I chuckled and looked at five flats of begonias, marigolds and lilies that needed to be planted. I got down on my knees and meditated for a moment and began to get my fingers dirty. I was intentional about what I touched, how I spaced the sprouts and how much water each root absorbed. I wasn't quick about it, I was intentional. That was the purpose of the day.

After almost two hours of the dirt, water and sun, I began to clean up my post. I worked in silence. For me, that's a real challenge. If I don't have anyone to bounce things off of, there's always a spirit nearby to chat with. So, if you ever see me talking to myself, know I'm having a staff meeting.

Nature surrounded and embraced me. The light breeze took the edge off of the beating sun. When I heard a voice, it started me.

"Hey, hi. How are you? Do you work here?"

Confused by his abruptness and noise, I shook my head no.

He stood next to the garden I just planted and admired it. "This looks great! So, is this where the guy killed himself?" I stood there emotionless, turned to him and said, "I've experienced several deaths since I met you, so there's that." I was annoyed that he was breaking my peace.

He persisted, "Did you know him? Is there anything you could tell me about him, like what work he did here or were you friends with him?"

I saw flashes of Haight and Asbury.

"I really don't know what you're talking about." I said in a monotone voice.

It dawned on him then. "You didn't see the news today, or they don't talk about it here? There was a man, a volunteer that set himself on fire here and died. A suicide. I'm from the Times Union and I want to tell his story. Make him into a real human so people can understand who he was."

I heard, "Leaving on a Jet Plane."

"Na Mu Myo Ho Ren Ge Kyo," I responded.

He looked at me confused and slightly mad. Then, in the doorway of the temple, Jun appeared with her hands behind her back wearing a ceremonial Japanese kimono.

"Arigatou," she said while motioning me to come in. The reporter followed us like a dog with a bone.

We walked through the temple, ornate with gold inlay, pictures of Master Teachers, scrolls and decorations. We walked into her living quarters. A one room loft with a bed, table with chairs, large basin and a couple of appliances that dated from the 1950s.

She offered cantaloupe and plain yogurt. After being in the sun and working through the dirt all morning, it was the most delicious thing ever. She showed our new friend brochures about the plight of whaling in the Pacific Northwest and how it affects the indigenous cultures along the coast.

"So, ma'am, did you know him, the man that died. Did he report to you? Did he ask you for help and did you lock the doors?" This Woodward wannabe showed his true self.

I saw flashes of the St. Louis Arch.

Jun smiled at him and said, "His body is gone, you're too late. If you cared about him, you would have known he was in turmoil. You could have helped him, but you didn't. And now you disrespect him and chase his soul away. Did you want his clothes, his jewelry, his money? Because he did not take any of that with him."

Not understanding much of what she said despite her excellent English, he persisted. "But this could not look good for the Peace Pagoda. I have so many questions, like what's in that temple and why did you choose here? Anyway, I want to tell his story and I have a deadline."

I saw his dog and the road trip.

Jun and I sat looking at him. We each represented a different aspect of the world. This reporter captured the struggle of survival and the need to pull in the energy of everything else to validate oneself. Jun was the wisdom of knowing what to discern, to be oneself and still be kind. I represented the struggle of moving from one world to the next. I was becoming.

Jun smiled, motioned to him and said to me, "Time to share your gift, your wisdom. He needs it now and I know you see it."

I sat for a moment and looked at him. He was silent, completely confused.

"You're leaving tomorrow morning for San Francisco. You want to get this story in so you can head out on the road. You have the car packed, you just need your dog and a full tank of gas. When you get to St. Louis to stay with your friends, you'll find out about the job. You'll meet the girl soon after and it's everything you were hoping for because she is your best friend."

He sat there with tears in his eyes. "Yes, I'm leaving as soon as this article is in. How did you know? Who are you people?" He glanced back and forth between the two of us. Jun gently bowed to show the top of her shaven head. I extended my card. "Let me know you get there safely. This happened for a reason."

"But what do I say in the article? I have nothing to write about!"

"Tell them that he was released from pain, and we shouldn't judge his process or his outcome." I spoke.

In shock and frustration, he excused himself. Jun and I sat in silence.

Jun looked at her 30-year-old men's watch on the table and said, "4:02, time for prayer." We rushed back to the temple. I sat in the gallery. She addressed the scroll and began to chant. Her words were mesmerizing and poetic, the sound echoed throughout the hall. She knelt and prayed in silence. I'm not sure what she prayed for, but I know I wanted to connect to the man who burned himself, the reporter that was off to his destiny and also to Jun, to understand her wisdom. I sent them all peace and gratitude for being on my journey.

She stood up from the Gohonzon and came down to me and asked me to follow her. She moved a chair to the front of the Taiko Drum and motioned me to play the other end. I picked up the striker. It was thick and as long as my arm. I began to hit the opposite end from where she sat. She encouraged me to hit hard and up tempo. The guttural sound filled the temple. She sat feeling the air push against her face from the vibration. Her smile was palpable.

I was sweating and finding new rhythms. I was now working the two strikers and finding new reverberations like heartbeat grooves, and my reward was her smile. When my arms were giving out, I gave a triplet ending that made her beam. "Just like my father," she said as she brought her chair over to sit with me. "Arigatou, Arigatou, Arigatou."

Jun held her hand on her heart. "I'm so full right now." She was beaming. After a few minutes of watching me catch my breath, she asked, "Did you find what you were looking for today?"

"I guess so," I said with a heavy exhale. I explained that I was there for a day of atonement, that I wanted to be within myself. She nodded and asked again, "But did you find what you were looking for today?"

She went on to explain to me the purpose of living for every day. "At the end of the day, you write it all in a book. The good, the not so good, the details and the intention. Then, you close the book and put it in a pouch. You tie it off and put it on a shelf. There it will sit as you left it. Every experience, every lesson, it is yours. But you cannot change it nor relive it. It sits on a shelf as knowledge. Be grateful that now you 'know' what is in it." She was efficient in her words, her motions.

"I have masters, you have angels. Our path is the same. I come from the East, you come from the West. Meet you at the top." She took my hands that were in my lap and walked me to the door. She stepped back and bowed, showing me the top of her shaven head.

A few months later, I received an email from the reporter. He wanted to thank me for the confidence I gave him that day, because he started his dream job with the Chronical the following week. He and his dog made it all the way to St. Louis before his car broke down and a few friends got him through while he stayed with them. "Oh!" he said, "The girl's name is Olivia, just like my dog and it's going great."

Past, Present, Historical Witness

In the art of Reiki, you administer the calm and energetic balance through Chakra work and relaxation. Many times, messages come through and often, clients will want to experience both messages and Reiki. Reiki, in and of itself, is a conduit for messages and delivering energy on many levels. Many that practice Reiki seamlessly connect with the messages that are meant to come through.

I sat with Laura for about a half hour. The reading was at best, pedestrian. She was not disappointed or excited, but I could tell it missed the wow factor that I was used to connecting with in a reading. She was more interested in the Reiki session as this was her self-care day anyhow. As we began, the room dropped in temperature. It was early summer and at first it felt like the air conditioner kicked on. Only there was no air conditioner. I was working with healing symbols and balancing Chakras when I felt a presence. I'm not one to grandstand because I think you lose credibility with trying to shock. But when you feel someone walk past you and stand at the foot of the person and introduce themselves, you take notice that it is one hundred percent the real experience.

"There's a man." Laura acknowledged that I spoke but she was relaxed in the session.

"Who is Gideon?" I asked.

She sat straight up. "Are you serious? That's my great, great, great, great, great grandfather."

She sat in disbelief and wonderment. "What is he saying? I'm doing so much work with him and the family."

I connected with the work she was doing on researching the family history. Putting it all back together and most importantly finding the final entry to his diary.

"Oh my God, yes, that's it," she welled up as I told her about the church basement being safe keeping for his journals and his eyewitness accounts. It was a lead she was looking for that was attached to a very precious family heirloom, not to mention an historical document.

Her lineage patriarch was Gideon Welles. Not necessarily a household name, however, he had a front row seat to a pivotal moment in America's timeline. He was the Naval Secretary to Abraham Lincoln. He was witness to the Gettysburg Address and if it were not for a sour stomach, he would have been sitting next to him at Ford Theater on that fateful night. He was an eloquent statesman that owned newspapers and had served in several state and federal offices. He was brought forward by Lincoln to revamp the Navy.

The Welles family had long squabbled over the contents and ownership of his writings and other artifacts. Gideon was clear to me in the message, he was tired of such division. Fitting dichotomy for a man that led the effort to reunify a country during a civil war.

Laura and her family had long since taken in an historian that had built his entire career around Gideon Welles. He understood the dynamics of Lincoln's challenges, Seward's Folly and the inner workings of what the country was going through. He held the president in as high regard as Gideon did. Because he was the foremost historian on Gideon Welles, through time, Gary became friendly with his ancestors and Laura considered him family. They took him in as if he was the uncle to be cared for, with regular interactions and certainly holidays and celebrations. After all, he had no other family, committing his entire life to reading and understanding Gideon's life, ideals, actions and convictions.

Laura, in her quest to find the final edition of Gideon's writings, suggested we meet with Gary and connect with him to find a deeper connection with Gideon's work.

I travelled to Connecticut where I met Gary, Laura and her parents. He was a caricature of himself as he had a long, tapered beard down to his chest. He wore wire rim glasses, an undershirt and tattered pants that served their purpose. He sat in a rocking chair and sipped the concentrated orange juice right from the can, without mix and fully thawed. He was polite and nodded to greetings and pleasantries, but he came to life when I asked him about Gideon.

I asked him what made him chose to be an historian of Gideon Welles. After all, most historians tend to choose bigger names with deeper historical impact like Washington, Jefferson or Lincoln himself. He simply gave me attributes of a glorious nature and emphasized that Gideon was the witness to Lincoln's greatness.

He switched his demeanor and incorporated animated hand gestures and superlatives that painted the picture of the wonderful leadership of Lincoln and his adoration of a man who was leading a country based on principle and integrity. Gary allowed himself to go back to this time and expressly showed his connections to Gideon. He slipped back and forth from third person to first.

I felt Gideon brush past me, like during the Reiki session. I saw Gary's body react as I felt it. He continued to talk with great enthusiasm, about the points of Lincoln's accomplishments and the explicit pain he was in, as he chose to emancipate over negotiate. I could see Gideon sitting within Gary. Then, the knowing of what was going on, hit me.

"How long have you known that you are Gideon Welles, Gary?" I asked in a clear, concise tone.

Laura snapped a quick look at me as it all made sense. The Birthdays', Christmas'. All of it.

"I am," he said. The relief that came over him allowed him to relax his 83-year-old shoulders, as he glanced around the room with a sheepish look as if he had been caught.

A Right to be Wrong

After teaching Intuitive development for over a decade, I found the truth in advertising, that it truly is a course of self-discovery. Through a series of classes which covered everything from Guides and Angels to Past Lives and Crystals, you could begin to find where your 'gift' fits into your life. As part of the class, there was an introduction to Astrology. It was a fun exercise to discover your triad; your Sun, Moon and Rising signs at the moment of birth. I remember Renee was absent from class that week, but I never knew why. No explanation, and not a problem. Life happens.

A few months after the class series ended, she scheduled an appointment for a reading. She was educated and well-spoken. I always had the impression that she was searching for something that she didn't quite understand and was looking for it on her journey.

"No," Renee said again. For almost 40 minutes, I had been painting a landscape of a man, who was in the military and called himself her grandfather. He was from a family that had distinct military honors and a connection to a town in Georgia. I talked about a cemetery, the family reunion and the coleslaw that came in two ways, 'wrong' and 'spicy.' I gave her specifics. His name, Gerald Theodore. A big giant "A." Bright red and yellow dresses and that a connection was coming soon. I always stuck to what I got. It was clear to me and Spirit was adamant.

"No," she said yet again.

As she got up to leave, Renee handed me a check for the reading. "I like you a lot, but today, you were really off." I felt guilty about the money, the exchange and not giving her any validation. It shook me a bit that I was not on point, and I needed to explore what the disconnect was and why I would still be ok with the money.

A season had passed and Renee booked another appointment. I was like, "Oh no." I wasn't sure I could handle being wrong again. I appreciated that she would be willing to see me through as a human being, but this was also an opportunity to get it right. And that, we all deserve. On the day of the reading, I planned my meditation time, was clean with my diet and allowed time for me to be rested and ready for the connection. The message in my meditation was clear, "Every little thing is gonna be alright." Really, Marley? Now?

We embraced like old friends, exchanged pleasantries and I began protecting our time together.

"We bring in our bright light. We ask our guides and angels to connect with us as we ask for the messages to come through that we hope to receive. We do this work in light, love and laughter so we can become the best version of ourselves, in all the work we are meant to do. Thank you for giving me the opportunity to do this work which allows me to be the light of the world."

"Can you say your full name and include your middle name as well," I ask this in every reading.

"Renee Aloysius Smith," she said robustly. It dawned on me that the last time we met, she didn't know her middle name. I thought maybe THAT was the reason for not connecting.

"I have to stop you right here and say something," she said. I was worried the past reading was about to take center stage. "You put me on a journey that I'm grateful for." The tension eased.

"I wasn't there in the astrology class because you needed the time of birth. It ended up being a knock'em down, drag out fight with my mother, sisters and everyone else. She wouldn't give me my birth certificate. After a year of fighting, I dropped it, but I didn't want to sit in a class and see what I would be missing. I made the decision to go get my birth certificate myself."

Still focused on the middle name, "Is that when you found your full name?"

"Yes, but there's more. I discovered my whole family. I learned my biological father was Aloysius Smith and his second cousins raised me. He had died in the military and my mother was too young to raise me. I grew up knowing these cousins, but as it turns out they were really my brothers and sisters. We had our family reunion and visited the cemetery where my grandfather Gerald Theodore's headstone is."

"Everything you said in that reading was spot on, even the spicy slaw that burned my mouth for days."

I sat there speechless and marinated in the lessons Spirit gave me with this experience. First, the consequences of following a journey and one's path, can lead to uncovering things that are personal and deep. So be ready for anything. Second, know you can be a catalyst, even if it isn't about you. And most importantly, trust Spirit. Stick to what they show you. Spirit has a perspective that you might not yet quite understand.

Rich and the Numbers

Skeptics are commonplace when you're a Medium. On average, I'd say I see a couple a week. Either they come to a show because they were dragged there, or they come to you because they want to somehow prove you wrong. Most the time, they are simply protecting their own behavior and want to stand out in someone's path. Anyone's path. Then, there is good skepticism. This is the developed trait that is open to the possibility of spiritual influence but recognizes that there are people in this world that will con or dupe anyone. These types of skeptics are very important.

As a result, their skepticism often proves the existence of connection. When I met Rich, he was a 70-year-old widower. He had gone through the balance of life caring for his beautiful wife, Andrea. Andrea had been given a few years to live when she received a new heart valve, the first in the country. Not yet 30 and a nurse herself, she knew the odds and struggles she would have. Rich became the husband she needed him to be. In his reading, she talked about how proud she was that he was sober all these years and her love was truly connected from the other side. It was an evidential reading where specific and quantitative things were presented to me and conveyed in the reading. When it comes to true evidential mediumship, the phrase most often said is, "There is no way you could have known that."

My journey with Rich only began with an impactful reading. He did, without a doubt, understand the power of connection.

He lost his best friend and the main reason for his day. His life was built around taking care of Andrea. Now, she was gone. Finding her in spirit was the next part of his journey.

When he showed up for Intuitive Development classes, he would blurt out, "I don't know what I'm doing here, but I'm here." It's common for people to think that they can't compare to a Medium, so they diminish their own ability to connect. Developing intuition allows students to be exposed to and try many modalities. Angels, protections, pendulums, Tarot, astrology; the list spans across the spiritual guidebook of becoming.

It was the fifth class and Rich was very lost in all of it. Grief will do that too. It makes you walk like a zombie and wish you would wake up from your nightmare and your person would be there again. Like nothing happened.

"I really like you Brandon and you talk about interesting stuff, but this just isn't for me. I don't get it."

"Give me one more class and if it doesn't make sense, then I will completely respect your process."

What Rich didn't know, was his wife Andrea had been showing me numbers. All the time. The fifth class was about numerology. I knew if it was going to click, this was the class.

Rich was intent, listened, responded and made sure he was getting the concepts of 1 being a new beginning, 2 being unity and so on. Even if this was his last class, he was going to absorb it as best he could. At the end of class, he shook my hand and said he had to think about next week.

The following week, I saw him pull in about 15 minutes before class, but he was ten minutes late coming in. He looked bewildered but calm.

"I was looking for a reason to leave, I really was. I didn't think I needed to be here for these classes. I pulled out my check book to do some balancing as I always do before class. There it was! My birthday is August 7th and here is September 9th. So, I always look for 7, 8, 9 in some combination. Well, I'm balancing the checkbook like I said and wouldn't you know it, there is 7, 8, 9 in the balance number."

The class was warm to his epiphany. It was the type of encouragement a group of empaths would cheer someone on in healing.

"But wait, there's more. I went back and realized, every time I was here for class and I would have 7,8,9 in some combination. Every WEEK!"

I smiled. The class congratulated him and encouraged him to keep going. Then I reminded him that the address here was also a sign. "Welcome to 987 New Loudon Road." The class sat with their mouths open. Rich closed his eyes and put his hand on his heart.

Rich went on to volunteer with bereavement services and the local National Cemetery where Andrea is buried. He talks to visitors about the signs from loved ones in passing. The eagles that fly overhead, the meaning of the coins on the graves and of course, the numerology of the dates and plot numbers. He took his loss and turned it into helping others. I'm proud to know him. Andrea is proud to be his guide.

Pam's Path

What if you had to power to heal someone from all their pain? The physical and emotional pain. The fear of knowing what is to come. What if they asked you with a look. The type of look that dilates the pupils, locks in on the crystal color of the iris and opens the window to a soul's purpose. I'm talking about a connection that releases you and them at the same time. A look that makes everything alright. A look that begins partly in desperation, partly in hopelessness but all human and all gratitude.

When Pam got to the hospital, the doctor sighed when he saw her. The grave condition from the emergency surgery was on his face. She was prepared for what she was about to see but didn't realize she was preparing for what she had to do.

His body was mangled. He was wrapped in blankets and bags of fluid hung everywhere. A nurse stood by the side of his bed and kept an eye on the monitor, checking her watch. She pursed her lips as intuition was telling the room what was coming.

Pam looked down at her husband through tear-stained eyes. Eleven years older, her husband was prideful about his independence despite the onset of Parkinson's and his body was simply starting to fail. She went through the phone tree in her head, the children contacted, near and far. Two were on their way, and the other was sitting helpless and stunned on the other side of the country. Knowing his father just had a horrific car accident and now everyone's biggest fear was realized, when he crossed over the double yellow line and hit a dump truck head on. Pam's thoughts were with her son and the helplessness he felt. She too could feel it.

The tube looked shoved into his mouth and out of place. She stood over him as the team of doctors came in. There's no such thing as bedside manner in life and death. The doctor was blunt and without remorse. "The legs aren't worth saving if I can't wake him up. He's not stable and beyond critical. They took extreme measures in the ambulance and he's here because of it. I'll be honest, we are keeping him comfortable until you tell us what to do."

She heard his words. They faded over the course of the conversation and began to sound like the "Peanuts" teacher talking, "His bladder ruptured on impact and his rib cage broke away at the sternum and now we wah wah wah wah wah..." She closed her eyes and let it hit her.

They met by chance and she remembered the tall, clean-cut gentleman with a checkered shirt and impeccably combed hair come to the door. They talked about her two small children and he lit up as he talked about his son. Their conversation turned toward how life hadn't quite happened the way they would have wanted, but neither would change any of it, as they wouldn't trade in their children for the world. They found comfort on their second chance and most importantly, found love beyond their challenges. He was wonderfully loyal and Pam felt compelled to take care of him in ways she never thought possible. Not as a wet nurse or care giver, but as a woman that felt pride in a man that wanted to make things right in his life.

The doctor snapped her out of it when he took her hand. "Ma'am, we need to know how far you want us to go with him. He's fragile. He's in pain. We have to take steps now to..."

"I know," she cut him off.

"I need a few minutes alone with him."

"Ok. But his nurse needs to monitor him." The doctor and the other white coats left. Pam walked up to her beloved and took his free hand, as the other was in a sleeve. She took it with both hands. He was in an induced coma and the tubes were keeping him alive as his tired body reacted to what was happening. She began to speak with a clear voice. A voice that he helped her find.

"Harold, I need your help right now." She positioned her lips to his good ear.

The nurse acted busy as if not to intrude. She stood idly staring at the EKG scrolling in front of her. She couldn't really see as the tears welled and rolled from her eyes. Her hands pressed buttons on machines that weren't on, but she never wiped a tear away. It's part of what made her an amazing nurse, and that what you learn is never taught, never wipe away a tear in the room.

Pam held his hand and was bringing warmth to his bones. She spoke again and said, "Do you know how wonderful you are?"

His eyes opened.

The nurse gasped as she looked at the monitor to see if the indicator that meant he was in a coma had changed. Despite the blip, his eyes were open.

Pam nodded her head yes and looked into his eyes. The nurse took a deep breath and knew the write up was coming as she walked out of the room. She knew this patient was in good hands.

"You've been through so much. This body," she said.

His eyes got wide. She stared into them. She saw how they met. How they romanced. How they lived and how they were happy. She saw how much her path and purpose was found in being with him. Partners, lovers and their soul connection. He began to squint and move his eyebrows like he was telling a story. Pam kept hold of his hand and said, "Yes, yes, I know."

He gently closed his eyes. As if to say, end of message.

The doctor came in mid reprimand of the nurse for leaving her post and exclaiming, "What do you mean he opened his eyes!"

Pam looked back at the doctor and froze him in his tracks. She had a sullen look and turned to the nurse. "You should be in charge here," letting her know that humanity trumps the rules.

"He told me it's time. He wants to go. He's been through enough."

Their many years of medical school meant nothing now. The only thing left for them to do was administer one medication and turn off one switch. Mechanical.

Pam watched the nurse's hand tremble as her thumb pushed the syringe of fluid into an IV line. Her schooling was real as she let tears fall from her face. Pam reached up and took her hand and let her know how grateful she was in that moment.

Pam saw her beloved's body finally rest as the morphine coursed through his veins. The machine pumping air into his lungs stopped and Harold's spirit floated above the room and saw his son put his hand on his wife's shoulder. Family.

As Pam looked into my eyes during the reading, I simply said, "Thank You for knowing I told you to let me go. It was my time and YOU gave my soul comfort."

Pam received validation that she connected and heard her husband's wishes. More importantly, it was her soul's work, her mission and her duty as a soul mate to hear and convey that message.

I closed my eyes and said, "End of message."

Soul Nesting

Alzheimer's is a debilitating disease. It's progressive in nature and depending upon treatment, it's only a matter of time instead of if or when, it gets the better of your body. When I was approached to meet people, whose parents had been diagnosed with Alzheimer's and were participating in a study being performed, I recognized it was an honor to begin to understand how a disease like this affects the soul.

My part would be to sit with the person in the study and read them. In an overgeneralization, it was a series of reading people who had Alzheimer's in various stages. They were all north of 70, some were even into their 80s. The conversations almost always streamed from a trance like connection. At first, they would struggle to find the words. I would sit and deliver my mantra to connect our Spirits together. They would connect easily as their loved ones would come right through.

In contrast, someone with dementia, could be combative and defensive. Alzheimer's and dementia are both diseases of the soul. They both occur in the later years of one's life and their minds are detaching from their body. More importantly, their soul is leaving their body. Your life path shows you how you are going to leave. How you handle your exit may also be influenced by how you've lived.

With my focus on Alzheimer's patients, I found that they would connect with people who were not only important to them in the present, but also with their extended lineage. Not just their grandparents, but also their great aunts and uncles, their second and third cousins, and their schoolmates from ages ago. And more often than not, I would consistently see a setting where they were being welcomed to an event like a family picnic or Christmas party.

I would share with them the settings and they would instantly know what I was talking about. For a long time, I thought it was because that was their favorite memory of yesteryear. I slowly began to realize it was where they went when they left their body and connected with their loved ones. Their body was breaking down but their soul was beginning its journey. I also realized that there was a term for this, soul nesting.

In the process of soul nesting, you begin to take inventory of everything in your life. The good, the bad and the opportunities you may have left on the table. It's a review of what you have done in your life. You look at your strengths, weaknesses, what you missed and what might have made you afraid. Many are able to celebrate their joys with the connections they had. And when they were faced with heartache or disappointment, it gave them perspective to know that they learned from it or understood how valuable it was to have experienced it. It was in a way, "This is Your Life." People who have had a near death experience, describe it as their life flashing before their eyes. We don't understand time on this plane. Someone suffering from Alzheimer's has extra time, as in soccer. We still don't know when the time will be up, but you have a little more time to process and a chance to get things right. We utilize time, we are slaves to it, but we don't understand it. There's something to be said about experiencing many things at once. We are then able to comprehend and understand them for perspective and healing.

In my opinion, the result of the study showed that people with an Alzheimer's diagnosis, would leave their bodies and their souls would have an experience with their loved ones on the other side. Their loved ones welcomed them and prepared them to understand their next step. The soul nesting they experienced, helped them understand their life's work and value. They could evaluate and make amends for any actions or regrets they had. Soul nesting time is about reconciling your soul contract and the people in it with you.

The milestone of death has always been respected. But to know there is a sea of loved ones waiting on the other side, I understood how healing and cathartic it could be. These weren't hauntings or warnings. These experiences were acts of love. The opportunity for spirit to show you how much they still loved and cared for you, and that they don't want you to be afraid of the next chapter. They don't want you to fear the inevitable. They want you to know that there was more to your soul than your body.

There were several readings that I sat with, but one was both unusual and reverberated deeply with me.

Emma Jeanne described her parents, her grandparents and her aunts and uncles. There was her sister, her nephew and of course her husband.

"We were sitting in this park and smelled the food. It was a big picnic. A celebration for nothing more than being together." She closed her eyes and imagined herself in her experience again.

I could feel her husband. "Lionel... Did he work at the steel mill?"

"Oh yes, that's him. Definitely."

I connected the dots of their home, their livelihood and their four children.

"David says he is at peace."

"How is my David?" She smiled and teared up instantly. "He was there, I know it was him, but his back was turned." Her 86-year-old eyes came to mine. "He is ok, yes? Yes?"

"He's sorry that you found him. He's sorry that he wasn't able to stop hating himself."

"But I loved him, I saw him. I didn't care about his boyfriend or anything else. He was my baby."

Sylvia, Emma Jeanne's daughter, sat up in her chair. "That's my brother. He still lived with my parents when he died of an overdose. The world was cruel to him. She says she doesn't want to die because she doesn't want to face him. She thinks she failed David."

Emma Jeanne's eyes glossed over. She began to speak off to the wall. She didn't complete sentences and her facial expressions were of surprise and joy. She left her body, if for only a moment. Then she said softly, "I see you, always have."

She came back into her body and was surprised they had a guest. "Janice, give our guest some, some, some, lemon water. Put out the sugar cubes." Janice was Sylvia's sister, who wasn't there.

I thanked her for her time and told her I must be going. I asked her how David was doing. She smiled and said, "You saw him too? He looked wonderful. I can't wait to hug him."

A few months later, Sylvia called to let me know that her mother passed. It was coincidentally (and there are no coincidences), the anniversary of the day David had passed. Twenty-nine years to the day. She described her final days as an emotional void, like she already left her body. She was not in pain, but not all there anymore. Hospice was swift but kind when the time came.

"All I can tell you Brandon, is that after that day she was at peace. Plain and simple."

Center Stage

Amazing things can happen in galleries. Messages from loved ones come through or validation of someone's path. But when a resident Spirit wants to make itself known, some incredible things can happen. Spirit uses what means they have to connect with you. The Studio's resident Spirit was ready to be heard.

The Studio was the summer home for a lot of gigging musicians who had a few days off and needed a place to practice. It had a place to stay, while in-between big paying gigs outside of Saratoga, New York. The previous owner was an amazing musician himself and had played with big bands. He played with orchestras that composed some of the greatest music ever made. When he passed, he left it to his daughter, Elizabeth. Elizabeth was an amazing pianist and composer in her own right. She was an accomplished teacher as well; having taught private students, and even big names that needed to brush up on their technique. She had refurbished the space and wanted to return it to its former glory. She sunk her life savings as well as the labor of love in it. The upkeep for an 1,800 square-foot building with an open auditorium loft in stage lighting, was pricey. I had read Elizabeth years earlier and told her I was coming back. When I developed "Funny You Should Say That!," I brought it to this stage in the woods.

It was a December show and I remember all the trimmings for Christmas. She had some modest lights scattered around, but the center piece was a giant Christmas tree about 20 feet tall and it lit up the night. The studio was perfect, with adjustable mood lighting and speakers that caught the acoustics. The audience had just enough space to sit, but they could see everything. I had completed about 30 readings or so and had been given the high sign that we were past the two- hour mark, when I began to fade a little. I decided to finish strong, and I absolutely wanted to honor the space in some way.

Elizabeth sat with her son Elihu towards the back. She was more of a spectator than anything else. The energy of her father was so prevalent. It was immersed in everything that went on there and I could actually see and feel him. I felt the music course through me. I heard the Glenn Miller Band and Count Basie. I tapped my foot along to big band era players that wanted to play the blue notes of jazz from depths of their soul. The emotions of music and the reminder of a simpler time before synthesizers and electric what-have-yous.

I did have some idea as to what I was looking for. There was a portrait of Elizabeth's father, Robert, as a younger man hanging backstage, surrounded by countless musical instruments and theatrical garb. "Elizabeth, thank you so much for having given us the opportunity to be in the space here tonight. It's an amazing energetic *FEEL*," I said.

"My father would've loved that you were doing this here. He was a musician, so intuition was totally his thing."

"Elizabeth," I said, "why is it that I feel like when I stand right here," I pointed to the floor in the center of the stage, just slightly off to the left. "Right *here* is where I feel him? He's super strong in this specific spot. Was this where he performed? Where he said he wanted to be remembered?"

"You gotta be kidding me, I'm about to give you some heavy validation."

When Elizabeth spoke, you could hear a pin drop. She spoke into the microphone, and it was as if everyone already felt what we were about to hear. "Brandon, where you were standing is where I placed a strand of his hair wrapped in a strand of mine beneath the floorboards, when we had the space redone and upgraded."

A hair under a stage isn't something you would expect to be a highlight of a show, but it was validation of a wonderful space. I felt him as if he was standing there with me. It was fantastic how Spirit wanted it to be known how amazing this man was. A man who influenced and inspired so many, and was still able to, even in passing with nothing more than a strand of hair under some wood planks.

This showed me the energy of what was around me. To know that things and space have energy. It caught my attention through the music and the bond with his daughter. I continued to connect with him through the conversation of song, and the encouragement to maintain a space that had passed its prime and use. He was honored his daughter made her life's work into a labor of love around this theater.

"Some shows end. You have to get ready for the next one," I said at the end of my time. Elizabeth smiled and knew exactly what that meant.

Cats and Counselors

Y ou truly meet all walks of life when you are a Medium. The loved ones that come through are not always family members. When you have a high impact on the people that you connect with in your 3-D life, they may reflect their gratitude in passing and in spirit.

It is not uncommon for a teacher to have a student come through, or a doctor or nurse to have a patient send a message. You also cannot quantify the frequency of connection in the 3-D world with how they will connect with you after they have passed.

That is why the connection for Colleen was important to share in this story.

In the middle of reading, I saw a boy holding a cat. He seemed at best, socially awkward. And at the most, I questioned if he had a learning disability or some other impediment that would keep him from being 'normal' or would make kids his age notice the difference immediately. I said the name Christopher. Her eyes lit up and instantly went flush with tears.

"I can't believe he's coming through." Colleen said clearly. "This was the most difficult thing I've ever lived through. I can't believe he's coming through."

I went on to thank her for her kindness, her words of wisdom and her encouragement along the way. She was the bright spot of his day, at different times in his life.

Colleen was a counselor in a rough school district. She was often the support for many students when they did not find support at home. Multiple times, she stepped in with the emotional tools that they needed to help cope, strategize and feel good about themselves. Because their home lives never leant them a caring ear or words of encouragement.

She was a healer for the world that she lived in. She had tremendous impact every day. And while Christopher, who had too much on his plate too quickly by having a difficult home life and simply being 'different.' She saw him and gave him comfort. She brought him to peace every day and gave him a safe space that every kid needs.

Christopher was famous for having a senior picture with his beloved cat. This beautiful soul loved his cat so much that he wanted to remember it in a picture. Once other high school kids find your senior picture, it's all about where they were in that moment, that hairstyle, the physical prowess. For Christopher it was a shared moment of how he expressed his love and joy. His cat understood him.

Christopher made national news in the dawn of social media and the fire storm of an odd kid loving his cat, went beyond that of normal growing pains. He was made fun of on a national scale, with ridicule that only the strong would survive. No one deserves to live through becoming a punchline in the new dawn of awkward memes.

This was one of those readings that made you wonder what the fuck is wrong with the world. Sorry for the harsh, but very direct way I feel.

In their 3-D life, Colleen was a lifeline for helping him understand that his choice to have a senior picture with this cat and lasers behind him was a unique one of love and kinship. She recalled the many times that he broke down and cried. Breaking the rules, she hugged her student, invited him simply to be and feel safe, if only for five minutes. But she always knew the harsh reality was outside her office.

The ridicule of a different kid, the emotional imbalance of never being led to feel safe. Where a cat is his only lifeline of affection, Colleen showed him that humans could be kind too.

He simply wanted to thank her for her kindness. She let out all of the emotions that arose. Being a high school counselor doesn't afford you the opportunity for your own healing process when you're helping with a loss of the student family. In this moment, Colleen finally had her opportunity.

I often joke that the reading should be free and the tissues should be $50 each. In this reading I should've sold her the box. This cathartic release was so necessary and was a long time in coming. We discussed the coping mechanisms of a loss in a school. We also talked about the cruelty of the world to a gentle soul. I reminded her of her light, her purpose and what she was meant to do in this world. Because once again she was the only one that came through for him.

Unbalanced

"He said, "It's not a suicide."

Her face lit up as the tears poured out.

"I knew it," she said with the breeze and strength to fight back tears while finding peace in validation of her father's honor.

"He showed his brain went sideways dizzy… Like he did not know where he was… Trying to breathe… Stood at the edge… Too close… I hate everything… I tried to catch myself."

Lauren looked at me with amazement. She said it had been so hard hearing everyone rule suicide. "Things were tough, but that was not my dad. He drove me to school every chance he got. That was our time together. He did not drive me to school that day because he had to deliver to an old client. But he called me and said he loved me and that he would see me later that night. Suicide never made sense."

She went on to explain that her father had a condition that affected his brain and made him feel dizzy quickly. The only relief he ever had was from fresh air. When it got too much, he would literally have to sit or lay down. And driving was almost impossible.

I sat there with a stone-cold face. I could not imagine being barely 20 and losing someone she loved as much as her dad. It shouldn't have been in the headlines. Being a local celebrity for his business, made her name recognizable. Everyone knew it was Lauren's dad.

We began to talk about the people around her, her mother and her friends. The ones that completely understood what she was going through. Imagine being on the precipice of your young adult life and everything that you thought was going to happen, suddenly changed.

She was suddenly thrust into the position to be the strong one for others. Particularly her mother, brother and the countless employees that knew him over the years, and were in shock and disbelief.

"He said he'd never leave you. The hawk, the hawk, the hawk." I pointed upwards, she smiled and nodded. "The hawk appeared on the day of the funeral." She believed in all of the spiritual stuff, but now it was becoming real.

Her life had changed that day. She began to take stock of her life and who was around her. No one replaces a parent, especially with the relationship she had with her father. She began to recognize the outpouring as some people simply wanted to be grief stricken with her. Even though they never really knew her father.

She also realized that her life truly would move on. That her father would still be a part of her life. Sometime after his passing, she met a wonderful man that understood who she was. When I mentioned him by name, she smiled and said, "I know he sent him."

"I want you to be happy. I want you to be safe."

Show Stopper

Have spirit, will travel. I take a lot of pride in being an active part of the community and helping where I can. When I was asked to perform for a grade school fundraiser, I think I said, "Are you sure??" Mom's and PTA be damned, they talked about it and several made the suggestion.

The local Country Club donated the space and locals and regulars came out. I had history with the club. On top of it being only blocks from my home, I had cleared the space when the new owners came in. The land itself was a hotbed of energy.

About a year earlier, I had a field trip with a class of intuitive students and we psychometrized the space. Psychometrizing is simply reading the energy of the space, as well as its energetic residents. Notice, I didn't say ghosts. I'm not a fan of 'hauntings.' But I'll listen if you can tell me about the energy and presence of a person. I am committed to recognize those that have a high emotional IQ, and can sense the presence of an energy. In other words, 'I ain't afraid of no ghosts.' They aren't here to harm or even scare. They are here to be noticed, honored, and healed.

While reading the space during our field trip, we connected with a couple of energetic residents. They were corroborated by current and former employees. When we sensed distress, we let the history books let us know what was up. As it turns out, at the bottom of the hill the club sat on, were train tracks that brought slaves up from New York City. The edge of the Hudson River was a primary place to trade contraband. So yeah, there was mixed energy for sure. We blessed and freed the space of anything that would hinder positive energy and that began the relationship.

The fundraising show was sold out and my niece, Kayleigh got her first chance to introduce me as an alumnus of the school. She was headed to college and returning to see some of her past teachers. Quite the buzz when everyone found out her uncle was a Medium, but it is not like we hid it. I gave my "Funny You Should Say That!" speech flawlessly and I was comfortable for certain.

Themes often happen at a Message Event. That day, it was about never giving up. I met an artist who would have an art show she did not know was coming. She had almost put her paint brushes down for good. Another person was really struggling with taking care of an elderly parent, watching her spirit slip from her everyday as they became strangers.

I found myself saying "keep going" time and again. It is the subtle encouragement someone needs. Sometimes, I don't even know why I say it. But that day, I felt the need to say it constantly. Which leads me to a showstopper reading.

I came to a young woman that worked at the school. She didn't quite know what to do with her gift, but she had it. I see gift around people as a blue aura. Sometimes it mutes into green. Blue is the symbol of a healer. Green is the actual healing that someone is going through or can provide for others. She was feeling her way after her grandfather passed. His flannel, his smell and a clear message came through. "Get the damn tattoo," I said with a smile. She confirmed that she had been thinking of a tattoo since he had passed as a way to honor him. Sometimes there is an impact directed to the person I'm delivering to. Other times, there are showstoppers.

A showstopper is a reading that everyone remembers. Many people attend looking for a message or some level of closure. Others come to hear an amazing connection.

"I can't explain what I'm seeing so I have to walk you through it." I said, getting the agreement of a 30 something year-old woman, with a round, cherub face and hope in her eyes. She kept her hair simply, her clothes practical and this was an afternoon out with her best friend.

"They show me THREE N's and as they show me them, they turn on their sides like they become Z's as they fade into the earth..."

She sobbed openly, as I kept seeing her in my mind's eye screaming "NO!" over and again.

She cleaned herself up and I asked if it was alright to continue, she nodded. She cleared her throat and gained her composure with it.

"Those were my three sons, Nicholas. They were still birth and I only gave one name... Nicholas. I asked them to come to me today, I wanted to hold them again." She broke down again and was uncontrollable. I hugged her as she found a new reservoir of the pain she felt that day. No matter how 'spot on' you are, no matter how 'incredible' you are, this is still a very human experience.

She gathered herself yet again. Her best friend gave her comfort in a way that makes you think everything will be alright.

"I'm sorry for your loss." I said like an underwhelming asshole. I needed to press it forward. The room was thick with energy and everything I had cleared out, was creeping back in.

"They show me they are safe and they want you to keep going…"

She looked at her best friend and broke into a fit of crying laughter this time as they nodded at one another. "I told you so," her friend said to her.

"No matter through you or adoption, you are meant to be an amazing mother. They are telling me you have been an amazing mother to them already."

Show Stopper.

And her best friend, became a fantastic student of Intuitive Development. She was meant to help people by telling them to keep going.

Look Me Up

It's not uncommon to hear stories about crazed, maniacal or even slightly odd people. Many times, it is funny and out of context. So, I have to tell you the story about Mary, who by all accounts wanted me to become an accomplice in her husband's demise, but what she was really asking for, was help.

I remember the reading being very pedestrian. I talked about her mother and father. I discussed an aunt that she was close to. I also let her know that there was an outstanding stock that she somehow hadn't cashed in yet and her father was adamant about it.

She sat up with excitement when I brought up her husband Bob. "What can you tell me about good old Bob?"

"I'm sensing that he is the center of a lot of peoples angst."

I went on to tell her about the physical ailments that he had. She was excited again when I talked about the recurring cancer that he had been fighting for almost 10 years. I also tapped into his greed and his divisiveness. He was narcissistic and most importantly, was abusive towards her, her children and the clients of the family business. I make it a point not to judge, but if I had to categorize, I would call him a son of a bitch.

"Yeah," she said in her thick Boston accent, "but when is he going to die?"

"I know not the hour nor the place," I replied.

"Yeah, I get that, but I was wondering since I'm paying you, you can tell me. It's on me, not you."

"I'm sorry Mary but it doesn't work that way." I remember telling her the story about Edgar Cayce providing readings for gamblers and stock market traders and becoming very sick because of it.

"Fine. You don't have to tell me the exact date, but maybe you could clue me in on the time of the year or maybe how many weeks it might be. You know ballpark."

"Mary," I said with laughter in my voice. "I really can't do that ethically and I don't think I would want to do what you're asking me to."

"But again, you're not doing it. I'm asking you to do it. You know, just tell me when the next stroke is coming so that then I could maybe not be home when he needs an ambulance."

I genuinely couldn't tell if she was dead pan serious, being tongue-in-cheek or flat out, a sociopath. But in defense of an abused woman, she was in the hope of a good life with his death. I began to realize how desperate she was when she continued to talk about how the world would be different without him.

"Maybe my daughter will speak to me again. That son of a bitch told her the worst things imaginable. I never did none of that... none of it, but since he said it first, of course I did it." She wasn't making sense, but that is understandable. Her husband had made her second guess everything about her thought process.

"My sons got no good habits because of it. I should've left him when the kids were young. I should've gone back to my mother and father." Her accent was so thick there wasn't a single 'R' in anything she said. "My son knows all the tricks, boy, every one of them. And I'm really sure that he'll get almost all the money. They all know that I'm the bad guy in all of this, and they never listened to me when I told them what he did to me."

"Mary are you safe?"

"I've never been safe," she said with a low, subtle matter of fact voice.

It was the third time that Mary had come to me. Each time she was always looking for some prediction of her husband's demise. She had a good heart and a troubled soul. I can never fully understand why people's paths become connected as cosmic partners or even soulmates, and then have such a torturous existence. The only thing I can honestly surmise is that with this purpose, there may be great rewards somewhere in the karmic soul. It is still not an easy perspective for a woman that never knows when she'll get the belt, or hear her son curse at her, or have her daughter say that she wished she never was born.

Mary lost her husband the following spring. She sent me a thank you note that simply read, "I sold my stock, heading to Florida, look me up. Mary."

The Coffee Can

"Where the hell are you?" Sandy said into her cell phone.

"Ha! I was grabbing coffee. What the hell is wrong with you?" I could feel the sense of urgency from Sandy. She was way too grounded to let something frazzle her, especially preshow. Things were already set up when we arrived, the tables, menus, etc. The PA system was up in a minute or two and I scooted out to the parking lot to grab a coffee.

"All hell is breaking loose! The bartender just kicked out a whole group of people for being rowdy. When are you coming back?"

I sat there with my coffee, Sandy on speaker phone and asked Spirit, in no uncertain terms, what the actual hell was going on. We were post pandemic and people were starting to get out again. I found out later that tensions were running high and the venue, which is amazing, was so short staffed that their tempers were short fused as well. I had played there over many years in various bands and the owner Goose, was one of those stand-up guys in the restaurant industry. He always did it right because it always came out in the wash. He was wonderful to the bands and was an all-around great guy.

I had just finished filming part of a documentary about businesses coming back from the pandemic. He took the government's rules very seriously and followed them to a tee. He did everything he needed to do to stay alive when his doors were open. He had a gravy train of takeout orders and the support from the community was second to none. You see, Goose was one of those transplants from out of the area that everybody loved. He was from the Greater Boston area and everyone loves a bar run by a snarky Bostonian. It was like having Sam Malone and Sam Adams shooting the shit with you. So, when I heard he was kicking people out, I knew it was the perfect storm. He happened to kick out a longtime client and their family who I knew very well. I met them in the parking lot when I returned with my coffee.

"Hey sorry, you guys the troublemakers?"

"All I did was ask for a glass of water. I don't even know what I did wrong but apparently, I wasn't following the rules." I joked around with him and vouched for Goose being short staffed and while I apologized, it was his venue and his rules. I ended up meeting with the seven of them at a later time for a private party and it worked out perfectly. Spirit is always working, don't ever think they're not.

When I walked back into the bar, Sandy was out of breath. She looked up at me and said, "Buddy, I don't know how you're gonna pull this one off tonight, everybody is off the hook." Given this was the first event many people had been to after the pandemic restrictions were lifted, we all had a little getting used to everyone again. It had been Zoom for two years and we'd forgotten how to act around people. I took the stance early on to simply accept people where they were, and to deescalate any challenges this way. You wouldn't think a Medium would have to deal with something like this. But the reality is that this is a very human business. We are connected with our souls, in the meatsuit that contains us. It's built with anxiety, fear, expectations and even happiness. You never know what you're gonna get.

I assured Goose that he did the right thing for his venue and I respected him. Because I truly did. He was the guy at the end of a tough couple of years, and he was still somehow making it. That night I brought over 75 people to his venue and all he had was three staff. He was tense because he cared about it. He's one of those people that'll give a job to someone down on their luck, he donated to every school function, and supported every family that had tragedy in the area. He **is** one of the good guys.

That's why I was there. I wanted to bring the business back to him.

When I started in with the readings, people were definitely on full tilt. Spirit was flying and laughter abounded. When I came to a woman up front, she clutched her purse by her feet and I began to deliver her departed grandmother.

"I feel like she was a drug dealer, like she's some sort of pill pusher." She erupted in laughter as her friend shook her head and said, "That's her!" I connected with the evidence about her behavior, her liver condition and her responsibilities after she passed. I tried to move on to the next person, but I kept getting drawn back to her.

"Did you bring something of your grandmother's here tonight, like a locket with her hair or something like that?" I had literally been shown an urn and after some nervous laughter she reached into her purse, pulled out her grandmother's ashes and slammed it down on the table. "There's my goddam grandmother!" The most modestly priced receptacle, a Folgers Coffee can sat in the middle of empty glasses and half eaten wings.

The entire crowd erupted with nervous laughter as well as oohs and aahs. I looked at Sandy and she chuckled, "She brought her G-D grandmother, B."

I have to take a couple of moments here to explain that I have a responsibility to speak for the dead. Your past loved ones are not show and tell items. Their ashes need to be respected. Bringing them to a public event or even a personal reading, is a little too much. Please always respect them. I know they're no longer with their physical remains, but at the end of the day how you treat them is part of your soul path. Pulling them out for shock value is disrespectful. It's also hysterical, but mostly disrespectful.

I also met Jen and Jackie that evening. A mother-daughter team that were searching for their soul path. They were looking for their purpose. Jen is a very talented jewelry maker. Artisan work is very difficult to make a full-time living in. But that's what Spirit showed me. The two of them being a powerhouse of unique offerings that were soul driven and from the heart of creation. I connected the dots with their loved ones as I explained what was missing. They looked at one another then back at me, appearing almost as if they were looking for a sign of encouragement to carry on with the business, or put it away on the shelf and never see it again. It was a moment of inspiration and more importantly purpose. "Keep smiling, beautiful," was a simple enough statement, but one Jen's father said often. That was his message. This was their tagline.

To think that people are always searching for closure from a loved one that might have passed too early, they are only seeing part of the picture. Most people are actually searching for the direction they're meant to be most recognized and valued in. It might not have been flashy in terms of a reading, but it was poignant for a mother and daughter's soul mission to find joy in what they do together.

They called me about a week later. Sandy and I started to carry their offerings in the shop. I also got them connected with an incredible marketing person. Shortly after, they were branded and their sales began to take off. "*Saged in Fire*" is an appropriate name for their company. They are blessed to be on a journey together and I know they're going to make it.

Rainbows and the Unicorn

It had been a day full of storms and I was literally double booked. I was a keynote speaker at an event on Friday and Sunday. I was invited to that event the day after I signed a contract to be on a tour boat on Lake George.

I was weary from doing a show in Connecticut, then getting up early and driving up to Lake George. To make things worse, the adventure was riddled with downpours. So much so, I was almost late getting to the boat for the six o'clock departure. It affected some of the last-minute ticket sales, but it was still a pretty packed hall as we shipped off to ride on the lake.

Doing a show on a tourist attraction is a very different experience. First of all, as a Pisces I had never been on the water to do readings. It was a completely new experience and I felt ungrounded. I had to keep thinking that I was completing the circuit through the boat into the water. It proved for some amazing reads.

I began with a family who all sat together. I looked out over the small islands and tourist beaches. We talked about how their annual trip was different this year, but yet their grandmother was still there with them. I sat down with them as the entire hall could still hear and see me as I delivered her memories.

In a stream of consciousness, I talked about the women's resort that she used to attend, and the childhood memories of what it meant to be on Lake George. We also talked about the history of the lake, Fort William Henry, A&W root beer, and playing video games with the grandchildren. I was delivering messages to all five of them. I let them know that they would still have plenty of time to sit out on the front of the boat and reminisce, because that was her favorite place to sit on the Mohican.

The Mohican itself was rich in history. It was the second oldest seafaring vessel still in operation in the United States. With a retired naval officer at the helm, its sightseeing tours were actually a step back into history. An historical site for both the Revolutionary and French and Indian wars, Lake George was a key waterway to Canada. In the 1920s, it had been a sleepy resort town where artists such as Georgia O'Keeffe and playwrights with summer vacation homes, came to collect their creative selves. In the 1950s, when "family fun" was becoming a part of business, Lake George began to bloom for being a place for both daytime trips and extended vacations for families and beauty seekers. I even remember as a teenager going to Lake George as a post-prom destination.

So, you can imagine my excitement to have the opportunity to be on a world-famous ship, where part of my childhood was experienced, and to have my name in lights on the Lake George boardwalk. It was an opportunity I would absolutely love to be a part of.

If you've ever been in upstate New York when there's been a torrential down pour, there are the most amazing sunsets afterward. This day was no exception, as I came to a family that had lost their son.

"He's showing me eight, is this August or how old he was?"

The father looked up from the table and said "Both." His skepticism began to melt. "Your son is talking about the pizza. It was delicious, he wishes he had some now."

"Oh my God, I just couldn't do it anymore. Every single day it was about him and I just couldn't do it anymore." His voice grew in cadence as he spoke. His wife held a balled-up tissue to her nose. "I couldn't even go there anymore."

"He's showing me a G or a J. It's almost as if he's singing Giuseppe's and he's laughing about it ...... or Geppetto's," I said with confidence as I clearly heard "Geppetto."

"That's HIM!" The otherwise stoic father looked at his wife who had closed her eyes, smiled and nodded. She wanted her son to come through to help her husband.

"Geppetto was a family name and it was his middle name," he continued and gushed for a few minutes about his son, how he passed suddenly in a freak accident. He went on to say he didn't believe in ANY of this and he still struggles with thinking that signs from loved ones are a real thing.

"He is sending you signs always. Right now, he's sending you a rainbow." I pointed behind him and the rainbow covered the entire lake. He turned his head and saw clear as a bell, ROYGBIV. While the rest of the boat took pictures of nature's wonder, he buried his head into his wife's shoulder saying, "I believe, I believe..."

When everyone had their photo-op, and he had composed himself, he took the microphone and stood up.

"I never believed in any of this shit... Unicorns and stuff, oh, um, sorry, no offense," he motioned to me. "But when he died, I went to work, I wanted to pretend it didn't happen. I shut it down... ten years ago... to the day, today, his birthday... I didn't believe."

"I'm glad you feel the connection again, what did it?" I asked.

"His gravestone is a giant rainbow... I'm sorry!" he said up to the sky, then to his wife.

Little Red Riding Hood

It was the Sunday before Thanksgiving and the weather had begun to change from fall to winter. The holiday fervor was in full swing. Having had the last full weekend of "normal life" before the holidays, I put my feet up to watch some football and eat food I shouldn't. As a strict rule, I never answer the phone on Sundays. But for some reason, this call needed to be answered.

"Brandon, it's Sam. We need your help up here at the Crest. Elicia has gone missing. No one has seen her for over 24 hours."

All I said was, "Send me the address and I'll be there as soon as I can."

Sam was a student of mine through Intuitive Development. He took the classes because he wanted to heighten his awareness of the plants and people he worked with as an Herbalist. He was not only certified, but he taught at several prestigious Natural Medicine schools in the northeast. He was accomplished, knowledgeable and scared for one his proteges.

I had met Elicia a few times in the preceding months. She had come to me for a reading, and later some abbreviated coaching sessions similar to what Sam had sought out with me. She was curious and connected. She had little to fear and had the natural reckonings most have in their mid-twenties; disappointing parents, not ready to start a family and which direction should she go in. After working dozens of active and cold cases with the police (State, County, Local), this was a rare opportunity to be asked directly by the family and friends. Subsequently, it is why I can write about this.

I am not permitted to publish or talk about the cases I work on through the police or an agency. As a matter of principle, law enforcement at every level, never openly discuss working with a Medium. There is an undercurrent of ego, as there are some professionals that don't have room for Spirit in investigative work. There is also the need to protect an active investigation. It's also recommended to keep quiet so you aren't outed and become a target of the criminal themselves. There are some investigators that find the assistance valuable, and others who debunk it immediately.

I had taught intuition at the police academy and to first responders. I provided tools and techniques to increase Emotional IQ in both decision making and recognizing triggers. Often times, the fight or flight mechanism is introduced. A tense situation doesn't encourage you to breathe normally, to process by listening to nuance or to connect with Spirit in the heat of the moment. What you can do, is know what you are feeling. For a first responder of any kind, it is getting your lower chakras in order. The root, the sacral and the solar plexus.

The root is your family, so one needs to recognize the bias of your socio-economic factors, including race and class. The sacral is about your belief systems and commonalities, that might be passions or prejudices. And your solar plexus is the gut feeling. The highest intuition you have in a tense situation. That's what I focused on to show them intuition and help them be better officers. How to put their training and know how to use it in the heat of the moment. In short, I know what makes them tick when they are combing the fields trying to find a lost herbalist on a cold winter's night.

As I drove to the Crest Commune, I remembered thinking this was important. I also reminded myself that whenever I'm involved with a police case, I'm not solving anything. My role is to help the officers and Search and Rescue teams. That's it. Help. Not do. That is very important. I can't get in the way and I certainly can't allow my ego in at any level. Conduit only.

As I pulled up to the main house, there were already county officers there. A state police officer was setting up a base camp in the kitchen. I met Sam and Elicia's mother, Karen, who I already knew because of a prior reading. It was Karen's insistence that I was brought in. Sam, an investigative officer, Carolyn the steward of the land, and I went to Elicia's cabin about a thousand feet away from the main house.

Officers came out with a note pad and began to interview each of us before we went into the cabin. It was cold, so they were quick. One of the officers started asking me questions like, "How do you know Elicia?" "When was the last time you saw her?" And, "What are you doing here?" The group kinda chuckled as I answered all his questions. "A Mediumship reading, three months ago, and I'm here to help you find her."

"Who is Patrick?' I asked the interviewing officer. "No one," he quickly responded. "Wait, that's my middle name though."

The other officer put his hand on his shoulder. "First time working with a Medium or first time with Brandon?"

The interviewing officer scoffed, "Whatever man. We can all just go home, and he can find her." He dismissed everything in the air. My help, and the hope of a family that had a lost child in the woods. Everything.

The other officer took his hand off his shoulder and got tight on him. "Listen, this guy was on the Blacksmith case, he's no joke and Syndergrass calls him." Syndergrass was the oldest and most grizzled guy in the investigative pool. He was either well respected or reviled for being too old school. It was street cred to be someone he would call. Truthfully, he was a serious pain in the ass. His skepticism pushed me and made me better. My stripes had been earned by working with him.

We sat in the tiny cabin. It was 12 ft by 8 ft, but nearly 20 feet tall with a loft. It was simple and I sat on a stool that could be raised or lowered by twisting it up or down. I closed my eyes and described what she was wearing. I could see her in a canvass jumper. One that would cover her extremities and had a hood. She also wore a Boston Red Sox knit hat, with the 'B' fallen off, but you could still see it. She had layers on and a turtle neck.

The interviewing officer jotted a few things down. Sam smiled and said, "That's exactly what she was wearing yesterday." The interviewing officer tried to debunk the exchange. "You two talked already, huh?" Sam turned serious and said, "I understand validation and he just gave it to everyone. He had no way of knowing any of that aside from his connection and what he is the best at." At the very least, her clothing would keep her warm in the 30-degree night. But as protective as her outfit would be, extended exposure is never good.

I walked out with Sam and up to the main house again. They had begun to divide up search parties and strategies. Air support, ATV and the Ranger battalion were due to arrive soon. I decided to isolate myself from the discussion so it wouldn't sway what I may get. Remember, conduit.

I went behind the main house. I began to meditate in the softly falling snow that had just started. It was adding to the few inches already on the ground. Through this meditation I was moving from tree to tree. I wasn't walking, or even floating, I was moving. Swiftly. With a grey wolf by my side. I didn't feel lost or even the slightest bit scared. Next thing I knew, I was flying over the trees and seeing the flashlights bob back and forth and hearing her name being called. "Elicia!"

Time is really an illusion when you work with Spirit. It is a backdrop that fades away. I'm not sure how long I was out there for, but I was beginning to feel the cold. I opened my eyes and before me was the largest owl I had ever seen. He was balanced on a wooden fence post and turned his head to look at me. He adjusted his balance on the post as he showed his wing span. They. Just. Kept. Unfurling. Open. He looked up and with one stroke of his massive wings, he lifted into the sky. I could feel and hear the air push against the night.

I walked inside and asked for a map of the area.

The base camp officer, Sean, told me that the ground crew took it with them. Sam was in one of the groups and knowing Sam, he didn't have the map. He wouldn't want to be hindered by such things as direction or terrain. He was out in the night with a few of his students, combing the area that they knew well.

I realized in that moment, why I was there. Sam had gone out into the night to find his lost student. I was there to support Sam and be the mentor he was to her.

"Give me a good size sheet of paper, please." I cleared a spot on the kitchen table. Carolyn came with a cup of coffee, a jar of colored pencils and legal sized pieces of paper. "I think you're going to need these."

I sat with the blank paper in front of me. I took a sip of the coffee, grabbed a pencil and began to draw whatever Spirit showed me. I had a road, a brook and a raised cluster of rocks. I had an abandoned house, as well as other occupied homes. I started to draw footprints that ended abruptly. I circled areas and made arrows.

You could hear the ATVs around the house, the helicopter overhead and radio chatter with commands and directions.

I started to write in the upper corner: House(s) Wolf, Birch trees. 3:38.

I closed my eyes and pushed the map towards Sean. He asked, "What am I looking at? Where is she?"

He studied the not to scale map, and had more questions than I could answer. Sean had been a Trooper for just a few years, but we had crossed paths before. He was open to what I wrote down, but knew he had to convince the Syndergrass's of the world, what to go on.

He pointed to the house I had drawn. "Do you think she's at the house? This one here?" He pointed to the darkly drawn house near the elevated shale rock formation. He spoke into his shoulder mic through to dispatch. "Is there an abandoned house up beyond the mountain road?"

"Copy that, on it now. No footprints here, nothing leading up to it." The voice frustratedly responded, as they had been pulled away from their holiday weekend.

"I'm going to go." I stood up from the table, said goodbye to the officer, the family and the stewards of the property. I gave my qualifying statement to another officer and went to my car. I saw the time when I sat down. It was 11:52 PM. I had been there almost 3 hours and knew their night had just begun. I watched the horses gallop up the driveway and be directed into the fields lit by only the moon.

I drove home exhausted. I texted Sam when I got home.

12:33 AM

"Thank you for bringing me in, let me know when YOU find her."

5:19 AM

Test from Sam, "Just left the hospital. She's safe. Talk tomorrow. Yes, I found her."

It took another full day to catch up. Sam took none of the credit and provided all the validation.

He told me the search had been called off at 3:00 AM, due to the resources and the cold. They would resume at 9:00 AM the next morning. Sam was defiant, knowing full well this would likely turn from search and rescue to recovery. He told me how they visited the vacant house three times in their searches. They couldn't find any foot prints, so each party turned away and went elsewhere. By then, the picture of the map had loaded into his phone as cell service was terrible in that area. He looked at it on the small screen and knew the abandoned house was there for a reason. While they called the search parties back, Sam stalled them and said, "One more place to look."

He went where logic didn't make sense. He went up beyond the abandoned house, looked inside and called her name. He then went behind the house, down the small gully to where there is a jettison of shale that looks like stairs. "Brandon, she was right there, curled up at the base of the rocks. There were no footprints. None. We found her just after 3:30 AM."

A month later, Elicia and I sat and meditated. She told of a fanciful connection and how she felt like she wasn't in her body. She didn't feel lost or scared. She moved between the trees with a wolf by her side. She felt like she was moving through their roots one minute, then flying overhead the next. She and I talked about her struggles with getting out of the hospital. Aside from some hypothermia and dehydration, she was fine. She was required to submit to a full panel of drug tests that came back completely clean. She laughed when she told me because it's a running joke that Herbalist aren't supposed to ingest the crop except during the holidays.

This experience reminded me to be there for my students so they can bloom and of the very human moment of how to help someone on their path. My growth that night was sevenfold. Personally, I had just shedded a lot of people, things and misconceptions. I had significant personal growth. I think I was rewarded because I had never connected with an animal, let alone an owl, like that before when working with Spirit. Everything was fluid, like I was an actor in a play and the director just let me go through the motions. Recognizing my ability to connect with animals, particularly wild animals, was an important step for me as I remain active in missing or lost persons cases.

Two by Two

We don't do grief and loss very well in this country. Three days standard. If you're lucky, it's a day to travel, a day to comfort family and friends and a day to get back. If you're really lucky, you couple it with a weekend. And if you've worked at a company for a long time, they let you take vacation time that you already earned. Most of the time off is going through things, personal belongings and memories. Maybe it's pulling together an estate, selling all their stuff and dividing things up evenly, so there isn't a pain in the ass sibling that's going to throw it in your face every time your wear your mother's ring.

Even in grief, we are distracted. We don't take time to mourn and we don't take time to go through the steps that are right for ourselves. We become compromised and rush, like we do everything else. We go through the steps of the cycle of life. Realize that everyone has their time. Being a Medium, I've connected with every loss imaginable. From the pets that were grateful for everything in their lives, to the best friend that should have followed your advice. To the aunt that loved you like you were their own child and to the grandparent you were named after.

When someone loses their child, the emotions range from the purpose of their presence, to being crestfallen because of the lost potential and opportunities to see them become who they were meant to be. You genuinely can never help a parent grieve a child's death. You just can't. Know that what they need is compassion and understanding. They look at whatever your role was to their child as a moment of vicarious living. If you were their best friend when they passed, their parent will smile and have a toast when you get married, because somewhere in their mind, that was their child. Same goes when you become a parent, graduate, get a promotion and when you become a grandparent. It is what they have, this timeline that you are showing them.

When you lose a spouse, it is an indignity all its own. When a spouse passes, the emotions range from regret to isolation. If their passing is while you are young, you can start again. That doesn't diminish the pain or the potential of a life lost. The reality is, trying to kick start a new relationship in your 20's or early 30's is almost common place. And if you lose your betrothed in the later stages in life, you can look back at all that you both created in the life that you built together.

But when you are mid-drift in the flow of life, it's considered a blend of tragedy and heartache. Because not only is the spouse alone, the kids had a relationship with them and it meant something. Somehow, getting over that hump in life is tough. You have to tighten your belt, but you do it to take care of your family, your kids and your future. You move toward that place where you can see the light at the end of the tunnel. You survive by finding that place where the little things in life made you the happiest. That's what you strive for, only you are alone.

You miss the things you promised one another that you would do together. Sitting on the back porch to watch the sun set. Listening to your kids laugh and play in the other room together. Splitting a pint of ice cream and laughing about dueling spoons. Stealing a minute in the bedroom before any of the kids know you're missing. Quoting your favorite movies and finishing one another's sentences.

Boom. Gone.

The financial turmoil. The loss of a role model for your kids. Missing the person that gets all your jokes. And oh yeah, the bed is too big in a hurry.

In whatever way people have come to me, when a widow under 50 needs a reading, it is when I need to be more than a Medium. There is a need for a plan. The self-reflection of what life looked like when you were truly content, versus the moment you became a single mother with burdens, responsibilities and grief in the highest order. When I met Tara, the shock of the loss of her husband was just the tip of the iceberg of what my role was to her and her family.

Our video reading was less than ideal, but it was mid Covid. When we set it up, I knew above all else, there was a need for healing.

"He's talking about one into two, like two by two. Are your kids Gemini's?"

"Well, we have two sets of twins, one of each… each time. He would always joke that he could make one of each, every time."

"He's showing me J's and M's."

"Jillian and Jeremy. The two younger ones are Sean and Sophia."

"The younger boy, that's me."

"Yes, Sean's middle name is David. He was named after him. Sophia is Lynn, after me."

The reading unfolded a life built between two people that loved one another immensely. Their hopes, their dreams and their children.

"Sean… he has dreams with his dad in it. If I was sitting with Sean, I would tell him that this is really special because his dad decided to come to him in dreams."

"Sean is most like his dad." The tears welled up in Tara's eyes with almost every topic.

I didn't realize it until I played it back, but I was acting like a mentor to her kids. Aged 12 and 16, the things I was saying, echoed what David would have said. This was him saying these things. It was part pain and part relief.

"Sophia wants to be a ballerina or an engineer, there's no in between!"

"Oh yes!" Her mother exclaimed.

"And what's the deal with fried chicken and macaroni and cheese?"

"He lived down south for over 20 years, he was in the Navy."

"Wait, Norfolk?"

"Oh yeah, Norfolk"

"That's where I was born, so now we know why he is ok with me being the one to deliver these messages. I'm a Navy Brat."

She looked at the screen and I knew she felt him, the words he said through me.

We talked for over an hour. We talked about faith, partnerships and family.

"Do you have a heart on your sleeve like a shirt, made for him?"

"No, but I'm thinking about getting a heart tattoo on my wrist. It's like a mirror or a picture inside the tattoo."

"It will be two hearts, one inside the other. It's from the ee Cummings poem."

I had invited her to take classes to help distract her, or help her understand how Spirit works. I'm not sure she really learned anything but she had something to look forward to every week, even for just a few hours. It gave her a reprieve from needing to sort through the abandonment she felt, through the finances, being the emotional support for four great kids and the realization that she was still alive and had an entire life in front of her. It was devastating and tiring. We talked regularly and it was sometimes the only normal time in her day. Her grief was realizing how much she had to do alone. The least I could do was be a friend and I offered her a chance to talk, any time. One day, we met for lunch and she couldn't wait to be seated.

Tara peeled back her sleeve and showed me her tattoo. It was heart, inside a heart.

<u>i carry your heart with me</u> by ee Cummings

i carry your heart with me(i carry it in
my heart)i am never without it(anywhere
i go you go,my dear;and whatever is done
by only me is your doing,my darling)
i fear
no fate(for you are my fate,my sweet)i want
no world(for beautiful you are my world,my true)
and it's you are whatever a moon has always meant
and whatever a sun will always sing is you

here is the deepest secret nobody knows
(here is the root of the root and the bud of the bud
and the sky of the sky of a tree called life;which grows
higher than soul can hope or mind can hide)
and this is the wonder that's keeping the stars apart

i carry your heart(i carry it in my heart)

The Golden Calf

When traveling from home party to home party, it's important to find time for yourself. It can be lonely when you're in the car alone for a few hours, then be on point for a message circle and travel back again. Really lonely. I came to realize that it was also a great place for self-care. I found a Shrine in Auriesville, named after St. Kateri. Whenever I would be in that area I would stop by, if even for a prayer. It had a beautiful cathedral in the round. Mass would be said facing different directions, depending on the feast celebration. The space had only natural light due to a tiered roof with windows. The pews, alter, pillars and accents were all wood.

I had a few hours before a home party and stopped by the chapel. What does a Medium do in a church before a home party? Well, he prays. He thinks. He replays things in his head that he could have done better. Sometimes it's remembering a memory from nine years of Catholic Schooling. Sometimes, it's thinking about how long I will have my parents. Other times, it's just nothing.

I was deep in thought about Sister Mary Knucklepants and the pain in the ass I was to her, when I was interrupted by the nicest of people. "Excuse me, I was wondering if you could help me? I'm doing the rosary. I haven't done it for a long time. I'm trying to remember how it goes."

"Did you just convert?" I said with a chuckle.

"No, but I'm terribly out of practice," she said like a child confessing bad news.

"Well," I said taking the plastic beads from her. "We start with the Apostle's Creed. Then, this here is of course, the Our Father." Holding the crucifix, I began to recite it and she followed along.

"Our Father who art in Heaven, hallowed be thy name…"

I was in a shrine, praying out loud, with a stranger.

"Then these three here, they are Hail Mary's." We began in unison, "Hail Mary, full of grace, the lord is with thee…"

"Then this medal in the center, this one is a special prayer." She listened intently as she was both remembering and learning what to do.

"Two all-beef patties, special sauce, lettuce, cheese, pickles, onions on a sesame seed bun."

She looked up at me and burst into laughter. Her cherub smile broke the dryness of my joke and her body moved with her waves of laughter. "I knew there was a reason I should ask you. I felt badly interrupting you because it looked like you were talking to someone. Angels or something?"

"No, I was just having a staff meeting. And I was doing what you were doing, thinking about your mom. Adeline, was it?" She looked at me for a minute and used her right hand to wipe tears off her left cheek. "That was her middle name. Did you know her?"

"She loved that you took care of her. That's why she will forever and a day, call you care bear."

She couldn't hold back. She started crying. "She came to me in a dream and told me to go pray the rosary. I went to three churches and they were all locked, for no reason! I used to tell her I did it all the time, but I just drove around the corner and usually got an ice cream." She laughed through her tears. "My name is Karen."

Karen began to talk about her mother. The details that really didn't matter much but meant everything to a memory. Her illness, her father, the way she loved macaroni and cheese. "I lost mom just before Christmas, two years ago. And then two weeks ago, I lost my cat. He got me through everything. Everything."

Part of me wanted to continue my lesson of the Rosary and discuss the meaning of each section, representing the Mysteries of Joy, Sorrow, Glorious and Luminous. I wanted to give her answers in the form of a question, like on Jeopardy, and tell her about Pope John Paul II's adoration of the rosary. I wanted to talk about how Mala beads were the inspiration for the modern Rosary, as they were atonement measures for prayer and time. But instead, I just listened.

I listened to Karen's adoration of her cat. A life devoted to the fluffiest, oversized purring calico that was rescued by the gentlest of prayers.

"Yeah, Big Mac used to sit in the window and wait for me to come home. Then one day he wasn't in the window. I couldn't bring myself to even look for him. I found him on my pillow because he needed me."

'Wait, did you say Big Mac?"

Her face lit up. We said in unison, "Two all-beef patties…"

"I used to sing that all the time."

I gave her my card, for whatever it was worth to her. Spirit had directed her and I to connect that day. It was healing for both of us.

As part of my visit, I would drive around the grounds. There was housing for Franciscan seminaries and large Pieta Statue that I was always in awe of. Frequently, I would find a priest sitting in front of Mary holding Jesus after he was removed from the cross. It's probably the one imagery that still moves me. Not the pain of man hanging from a cross from a barbaric act. Not a statue of a Saint dripping in symbolism. But the statue of a mother holding her son just after he died. The mortality of holding him just after he was born, then just after he died, makes the whole God thing, well, human.

Subsequently, the Catholic Church sold part of this land and the former Jesuit retirement home to a Buddhist Temple. In an absolute dick move, after the Diocese sold the property to a devout Buddhist community that believe in alleviating human suffering through meditation, prayer and consciousness, they build a four-mile fence from one end of the property to the other. It also cut the ONLY road in and out of the facility. It took them months to gain approval and build a new entrance. In a sheer act of forgiveness, the stewards of the temple went to the town, led the planning board in prayer and said they had forgiven the Diocesan leader (they specifically named him) and wish no ill will to their fellows in faith. Their request was expedited. A road was built post haste.

I still visit the shrine. It is an amazing place to find respite. But when I leave, I visit the temple as well. I also donate 108 dollars. The amount equals the number of beads a Mala has and represents enlightenment and atonement. Peace. The value is to know that your money has energy. You vote with your energy every day with where you spend your money, your time and your effort. I'm also following true leadership and honoring the energy of forgiveness.

Three of Cups

Home parties always have an odd set up. People crammed onto a couch and kitchen chairs in the hallway. And if there aren't enough chairs, someone will always pop a squat in the middle of the floor. All these options run out of comfort in a half hour. The link tends to be the person that arranged the party. They know me from a reading or a show, but generally I'm brand new to everyone else in the room. Most home parties are between eight and fourteen people. What I noticed after doing literally hundreds of them, is that there is almost always a theme. The same goes for public shows, but with a home party, the theme tends to be driven by a thread that weaves everyone together.

I often open with a series of caveats. First, that Spirit is gonna be Spirit. It does what it wants, so the message I connect with has purpose and I can't control it or change its intention. Also, I acknowledge that this is a public setting and if I ever bring up something that shouldn't be public, then they must wave me off.

The owner of the home sat under the archway between the living room and dining room. I smiled and began, "I know your sister was very important to you. Sheryl, Cybil. She gives me names like a starlet."

"She always thought she was a movie star. It was a family joke."

"She's talking about the family growing and how happy you are to be a grandmother." I held up two fingers. "Was there a twin?"

"No, but my granddaughter is upstairs now sleeping. She's 3 months old." Her daughter was sitting in front of her and looked like a new mom should. Slightly tired but loving every moment of life's changes around her.

"Rose is claiming your child, she said it was hers, but really it was yours." Sometimes Spirit spits it out at me, and sure enough I sound like a rambling mess. "That's my grandmother, we were really close. That was her middle name."

"She keeps saying congratulations and she says it twice." I was pointing to the mom in the archway.

I moved on to the next woman. I smiled and said "Congratulations!" She looked away like she had her hand caught in the cookie jar. She smiled and gently shook her head.

You can't shake off a catcher calling a sign when you're throwing a perfect game. I let it sit there.

She looked at me and said, "No one knows. I know it's time." She looked at her mother and sister, "We're pregnant."

The living room erupted in sheer joy. Her eldest daughter told the story of their journey, the miscarriages and failed fertility treatments. It was an eight year-long saga, but the baby was due near their ninth anniversary. Eight (8) was their manifesting, nine (9) was the end of that part of their journey. The joy turned into a counseling session, because the wounds of seeing her younger sister have children without trouble, was very emotional. The happiness of being an aunt, a friend to her sister and the pain of seeing exactly what she wanted, while not obtaining her dream.

"I understand." I repeatedly said. I apologized for foiling their Thanksgiving Day announcements and that's when magic happened. The plot was hatched. The younger daughter brought them in for the grand scheme.

"But Dad doesn't know, let's surprise him!" The three joined together in a plot that was not meant for an audience. They talked about what dad would really like to see and mom wanting him to earn it in a tongue in cheek game of charades. The plan was halted and I started connecting again. That didn't stop the ideas from flowing. It's also the reason why I plan on 90 minutes to two hours, but sometimes end up leaving close to midnight.

It was all worth it to see these three women connect on their life's purpose. It was a true celebration.

Archangel Michael, Pray for us.

I'm all about a fundraiser. I usually have a sweet spot for old friends and social causes. So having the opportunity to help a local Rotary chapter, was a blessing I jumped at. In upstate New York, everything seems to lead to somewhere, even when it's in the middle of nowhere. Historically rich, the state has pockets of 'George Washington slept here' signs along with 'On this land the brave regiment of John Stark fought Burgoyne's army." They are obscure references to slivers of history, while also being the claim to fame of these once booming townships that are now sleepy inlays of Americana. My friend was the President of the Sharon Springs, New York Chapter. It's famous for being one of the opening post cards in "National Lampoon's Vacation" and the Beekman Boys. It once was an attraction for the Healing Springs that were said to give youth and vitality to all that drank it. In the late 1800's to about 1930, it was a bustling midway between Syracuse and New York City, where you could stay at spas that boasted water from the springs for you and your horses. Shortly after the efficiency of automobiles came around, it became nothing more than a 15-minute pitstop.

Current population 515.

This fundraiser had always done more for the charity than it did for my career, but I was grateful for it. Where else could you have a Medium hold a message circle in a Free Public Library and open the show with, "A Medium in a library. He must be doing some reading." That joke retired on the 'ing' part of reading. Host Pam was always gracious and ready for a laugh. She knew the drill, being quite intuitive herself, and knew when to ask questions or get out of the way. Sandy was checking in the audience, while I sat in the back office with nine chairs. This was presumably where the town business happened. I put my feet up and rested for a few minutes. I walked out 'on stage' a few minutes later to find the arts and crafts/general storage room turned into a curved seat amphitheater.

When I first walked out, I saw lightening streaks shoot from one end of the room to the other. They flashed overhead and through the audience members. After saying my terrible Medium reading joke, I continued.

"I want to thank you all for coming out and supporting the Lion's Club today."

Pam cleared her throat and corrected me, "Ahem, Rotary Club."

The chuckle was worth it when they heard it was supporting the Rotary Club. Spirit had given me the joke; I was just following along. The energy shifted however, and I felt like I was being led somewhere, instead of following along.

The messages flowed like the healing waters the town was known for. Paramedics being told about their calls, grandmothers recalling their journeys from the homeland and the due date of a baby not yet on an ultrasound. The messages were on point, with evidence and had real impact on those that needed to hear them.

About an hour and a half in, a woman came barreling through the door. She knocked over the folding chair she was trying to sit in and was completely out of breath as if she had run the whole way. The energy of the room changed, but being a consummate professional, I knew how to manage the situation. Caitlyn is this beautiful, radiant soul that looks like a hot mess when she tries to defy logic and find a more suitable venue for a Medium. It was reasonable that she would look for a restaurant or a hotel, but instead, I was at a library. Her GPS brought her to a open empty field that would have been suitable for crop circles or a CE-5 Meditation.

"I'm so sorry I'm late. I got turned around and I was in, um, on the other side of town and I just couldn't find the road and then I was like, I'll find it and closed my eyes and I was here."

Grace is the only weapon when someone is frazzled. They typically have it together, just not in that moment. I continued on to a few other readings, and when I came to back to her, she was calm, cool and collected.

"I know you," I said. I always give disclosure in shows. It's authentic and moreover it gets us to the point we need to be on. I felt someone in Spirit walk in. It was white. White gown, white hair with a white aura. I saw the face of someone I knew a long time ago, from early in my work.

"How do you know Hillary?"

"She's my sister." She began to cry. "That is why I'm here. She's gone."

Here is a secret. Many people think that Mediums have it all together when it comes to loss. Truth is, it hits us harder because we think we should have seen it coming and should have solace that we can simply connect again whenever we want. It's not that simple. As a matter of fact, it's more difficult because the connection we need is through a person that has suffered the loss. It is a connection through psychometry; a house, a piece of clothing, a person in grief. Each has a different energy connected to the person that has crossed over, but they are the bridge to them. Therefore, we believe in the Merkabah (Flower of Life) in terms of HOW we are connected. When we know them personally, THE MEDIUM is the conduit. It's like hooking right up to the grid and drawing electricity straight from the source.

You could have knocked me over with a feather in that moment.

Caitlyn described how her sister passed. She contracted a rare and incurable infection. She transitioned from her body on 11/11. Hillary was a mystic. She could sit with you for a reading, interpret numerology, and would undertake large order missions, like translating the Voyanovich Manuscript and doing research for Dr. Steven Greer in Extra Terrestrial contact and disclosure. She worked with portals, time travel and was a librarian of the Akashic records. On her worst day, Hillary was fascinating.

But like most of us in the lightworker world, our ego can get the better of us while our journey gives us opportunities. I had appeared on her podcast and subsequently, I asked her to host a message circle at my space. Like many lessons I learned, business clarity was one of them. She was there to teach me the lesson of agreeing to terms before an event. She expected the full ticket sale without paying the house. It was a heated exchange of exasperation and disbelief, that she expected to NOT pay anything to a venue that brought in 18 people to her event. Hillary took the cash in her hand, without counting it, folded it and put it into her bag. "I'll tell you what, when you get your shit together, I'll come back," she said.

Those were the last words she spoke to me in the living. Here she was walking through in a grand entrance as only she would. She was radiant and looked at her sister. She explained that it had to happen this way. Caitlyn knew what she meant. No goodbye, just cut off coldly. Caitlyn and I had that in common with her.

I saw Hillary turn her head and say, "This is the one I told you about." I saw the translucent slivers of light fade and regenerate while folding into one another. It was the weave of an angel's wing. I had seen glimmers of it before, but never so fully. It was him.

Archangel Michael. ~AAM.

I could only see one wing and the hand that held his kyanite sword. Gripping it with ease, he was at the ready but not for a fight. I felt the rest of the experience. His easement of all the obligations in my life. The purpose that each challenge and person had in my life and why they occurred. Why certain people were in particular roles and how it all fit together. He gave me peace through knowledge. He showed me my mistakes were guided, the experiences had purpose, the people I helped and hurt, all needed me on their path.

Hillary was the conduit. The connector. Her sister, the link.

In his presence, I left my body. Completely gone. To those in attendance, they sensed something was happening. I wasn't coherent and was speaking in a language that was English'y' but I sputtered sentence fragments and was an emotional spillway. I sat down as I couldn't feel anything, which is exactly what was meant to happen. Michael was clear to me it was go time. Things would fall away and I needed to quit being so, well, human about everything. Enjoy the ride, it has purpose.

"She's safe now, she has Michael," I said.

"That is her son's name, I have no doubt."

"I have to go." Caitlyn picked up her bags and coat and walked out.

The room sat in shock, not really knowing what just happened. I took a drink of water so I could come back into my body. I couldn't feel anything. It was electric and magnetic. I still had more readings to deliver and I had to keep it wide open. I just started speaking. It wasn't me; it was the function of what I was.

"This child, no one knows."

She said, "Well, you knew when I came to you for a reading last year." The humor changed the energy just enough. I'm terrible at 'guessing' the plumbing of a child, but I can connect with their energy and their purpose.

"He's meant to bring balance to everything. Your marriage, your life and the world."

I paused to absorb the moment. "You are the Leo?"

"Yes!" She said covering her mouth. "That's also his due date."

"Oh, he's going to be a Leo too?!"

"Same as my birthday, August 8th."

I had to sit back down. 8/8 is the Lion's Gate. The portal to Orion's Belt. It is when the great pyramids in Egypt align with Orion. It is a gateway to consciousness, to purpose and an alternative reality. A message of hope, humanity and connection. A mother and child with a portal birthing. A certainty, not a maybe. Well played, Hillary. I hope you were telling me I have my shit together now.

Shiny New Penny

After learning how this business works, there's a deep understanding that people will always look out for themselves. I had a floundering YouTube channel for some time, when I realized politics sells. When you add in the relevancy of a path work specialty, like Mediumship or Astrology, you can form something unique. After the suggestion of a soul mentor, I pulled together the astrological chart of Volodymir Zelensky and talked about what made him tick and the resolve he would need as his country was invaded. It went viral and instantly created a whole new way for me to connect and deliver. It was a platform I had been preparing myself for my entire career. After teaching Intuitive Development, Mediumship, Mindfulness and being a Reiki Master Teacher for a long time, you find the tenor of your voice and how you want to present a message and start the discussion.

In the past, I made the critical and disastrous mistake of thinking that people wanted it as much as I did. I created a community that was meant to be an extension of teaching intuition and a platform for people to 'figure it out.' It was to be a safe space to be accepted and find purpose for your individual gift. Instead, it lacked the necessary boundaries for self-discovery. What the space became was fueled by my drive to elevate people when they said they wanted to bring their light to the world. What I found was an unhealthy world of trauma bonding and victimization. When challenged to do the work, many folded, blamed, or triangulated a situation that did not allow them to do the mirror work that was necessary for elevation.

I found myself always looking for the shiny new penny.

At that time, the model was based on taking classes, then elevating to a place to share your gift. By design, the community that came before you, would lift you up. It was to become the community I longed for as I was starting out. One that incessantly supported and cheered one another on, with the idea that when one of us was successful, we were all successful. After all, using your gift with Spirit was not something taught in school, or naturally encouraged. You're looked at as an oddity, an outcast. You're made to feel 'weird' if you connect with Spirit and help others. My vision was to create a safe space where we used intuition and kindness to help one another.

Instead, I found a cesspool of unresolved traumas, addictions and tortured souls that didn't take accountability and were ready to be the victim with every mistake made. It was unkind and without merit, not to be the lightworker they professed to be. They fell into the trap of judgement and condescension. They found comfort in becoming the gaggle, that became the angry mob that wants justice and punishment. At the height of the #MeToo movement and the Trump administration, anger was the tone of the frustrated. It was easy to see that the energy was ripe for negativity and dissent. That is when I went from doing astrology, to understanding astrology. I saw the energy shift and put the target on my back instead of people having my back.

Everything that made me great was used against me. A twist of a story, the tone of how I said something or using circumstantial timelines to make things look a certain way. It was a time ripe with the misappropriation of using Spirit. Instead of actual evidence, key phrases were used like, "Spirit told me." Or, "Are you getting this, because I'm getting this." And when put together, it's then real through the power of suggestion. Many took what little gift they had and turned it into the gossip and victim channel. My sin in this, was that I allowed it.

No one asks questions when the victim is compelling, sympathetic, loud and first to speak.

There were signs along the way. Whispers in classes, finding plot laden emails and being texted erroneously awful things I supposedly said. I guess I was akin to the environment, too. I made personal mistakes that I never would have, with the right footing and people around me. That's a feast day for people who want to triangulate in order to avoid their own path and responsibilities.

If you are paying attention to your own healing, when Chiron returns in your chart, you can make strides. When you address your shadow work, you can become whole. When you don't, you look to hurt people.

I began to dig deeper to understand my own Astrology Chart better. Self-awareness is the key to understanding ego. As a natural teacher, I saw the lessons and how it all fit together. Cycles repeat and each one of us has a story line to play out with the Astrological weather. It's not just an exercise in the esoteric, it is an insight to opportunities we are given with the energy that stems from our soul's mission.

Spirit always nails it for me. As my YouTube channel was taking off, I received many notes from other light workers, Astrologers, Mediums, etc. They appreciated my fresh perspective and the way I explained things. One message stood out and I knew I needed to flush it out. I saw she was an Astrologer and Life Coach from Malta. After being in this work for years, I found it hard to believe that I didn't know her or hadn't at least heard about her.

I quickly found out that she was not in Malta, New York, just a few miles away, but rather in Malta the country, in the middle of the Mediterranean. And she was English to boot! After a few jovial conversations, I realized she was someone who could understand the concept of how kindness and energy would be mutually beneficial for both of us. Our show, Whiskey and Bagels was born. It was meant to be a casual conversation about astrology that is current, while teaching others. It was a smashing success because of its authenticity, humor and insight.

"Hi everyone and welcome to another episode of Whiskey and Bagels. I'm conscious Medium Brandon Russ and with me on the other side of the Atlantic IS..."

"I'm Astro Life Coach, Penny Dix." It made me realize that she was the shiny new penny I was looking for all along. This was where I needed to be. Her knowledge of Astrology complimented mine, her sense of humor played well with my off-beat delivery, and as a trained performer in song and film, she has a stage presence that could match mine. I'm acknowledging that I can be a lot at times, and as a retired psychotherapist, Penny managed our connection perfectly.

When we were searching for a new idea to present the raw, authentic content we were building, we decided to review one another's charts. We filmed it as a special and by the end of it, we were both in tears, comforting one another. We saw each other's journeys. She showed me compassion and I offered her perspective as it became a confessional of mistakes, patterns, and pain recognition. We also saw one another's light, purpose and joy. By the end of it all, we realized that this safe place we made for one another, couldn't be broken and shouldn't be shown to the world. It was perfect timing for our paths to cross. We laugh together almost every day. Isn't that my mission? To raise the vibration with laughter?

I joked that I should at least, be sending her a co-pay for how she has supported me and jumped into therapist mode with my struggles. She would always say something like, "This will always come back to me. Helping you shine, helps me shine." She was validating the vibration I was setting for myself. I sometimes thought I was a failure for not seeing my vision come to light the way I thought it would be. But this exchange helped me form a new standard of any interaction both in business and in my personal life. I also had the perspective of those that helped get me here from the beginning. Those that understood the parts of me that mattered. The strengths and weaknesses, and they helped keep me modest.

All of these experiences let me hold true my compass.

My quote from my high school yearbook was, "I can divide my life into two categories, the things that are funny and the things that don't matter."

Funny I should write that quote 32 years before this book came to light. I need to start giving myself more credit for trusting my path.

The Final Page

There is magic in creating a book like this one. I've come to realize how cathartic it is to recall and recollect how you got to a certain place in life. What I was amazed at the most, was how many stories aren't in the book. I'd like to thank the cutting room floor for catching all the chapters that weren't ready yet for the world to see and "Funnier You Should Say That!" is already in the works. I remember the moments where I got angry, stayed angry and thought better of giving it a piece of my mind and space in my story. Clearly, I should do it again.

I also understood how many teachers I've had. The ones that were formal. The ones with scheduled times, homework, follow up and progress updates. And the ones that I meet every day. The opportunities to grow have been never ending for me. I thank all the people on my path that have helped me, hurt me, and blessed me. I've been that in return to them in equal measure; with the lessons that helped them, hurt them and blessed them. They are all important and I will continue to embrace everything as it comes and do it with laughter.

Back in 1991, "Funny You Should Say That!" got its first entry when my high school senior yearbook was printed. There, under my fluffy haired picture was "J. Brandon Russ." For all eternity, my first initial will be wrong. They swear it was because of my poor penmanship and to their credit, I do write like a physician in a rush. But it was my quote that really should live in infamy.

"I can divide my life into two categories. The things that are funny and the things that don't matter."

That's how I signed off on my high school career. I went on to attend classes at seven different educational hotbeds and they were all lucky to have me. I will strive to always be transparent and show that mistakes happen, and the circumstances aren't fatal. But where I learned the most was when I navigated the real world with a gift that I was meant to use every day. I've learned how to apply the awkward and sometimes crazy connection with Spirit as I found purpose with it, instead of fear. And we all know, the opposite of fear, is love.

Made in the USA
Coppell, TX
10 December 2022